POSSIBLE PALLADIAN VILLAS

(Plus a Few Instructively Impossible Ones)

George Hersey

Richard Freedman

POSSIBLE PALLADIAN VILLAS

The MIT Press   *Cambridge, Massachusetts*   *London, England*

POSSIBLE PALLADIAN VILLAS

(Plus a Few Instructively Impossible Ones)

George Hersey

Richard Freedman

This book was set in Trump Mediaeval and Copperplate Gothic by the MIT Press and was printed and bound in the United States of America.

Library of Congress Cataloging-in-Publication Data

Hersey, George L.
    Possible Palladian villas : (plus a few instructively impossible ones) /
    George Hersey and Richard Freedman.
        p.   cm.
    Includes bibliographical references (p.   ) and index.
    ISBN 0-262-08210-1. — ISBN 0-262-58110-8 (pbk.)
        1. Architecture, Domestic—Data processing.   2. Architectural design—Data
    processing.   3. Palladio, Andrea, 1508–1580.   I. Freedman, Richard, 1964–
    II. Title.
    NA7125.H47   1992
    728.8'092—dc20   91-30077
                                                                              CIP

There is a Macintosh program that can be used with Possible Palladian Villas. It allows the user to design Palladian villas by applying the rules described in the book. It requires 512K memory, runs on any Macintosh system, and is compatible with System 7. For more information, please contact Sales Department, The MIT Press, 55 Hayward Street, Cambridge, MA 02142 U.S.A.

To Nancy Freedman and Samuel Ashton Hersey

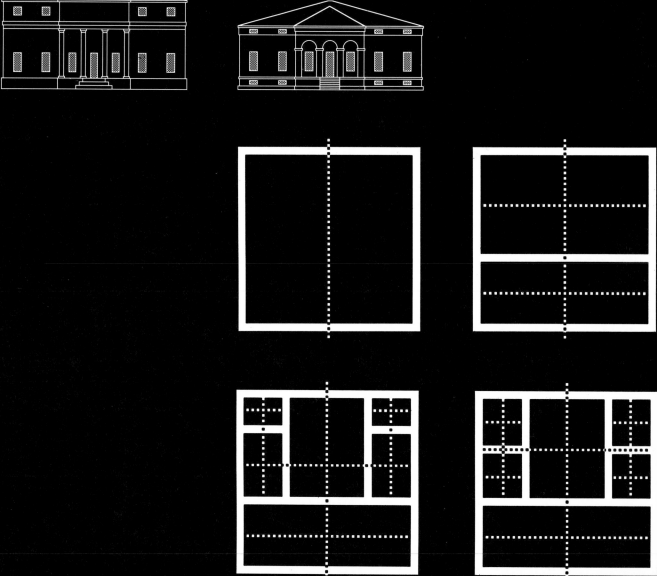

CONTENTS

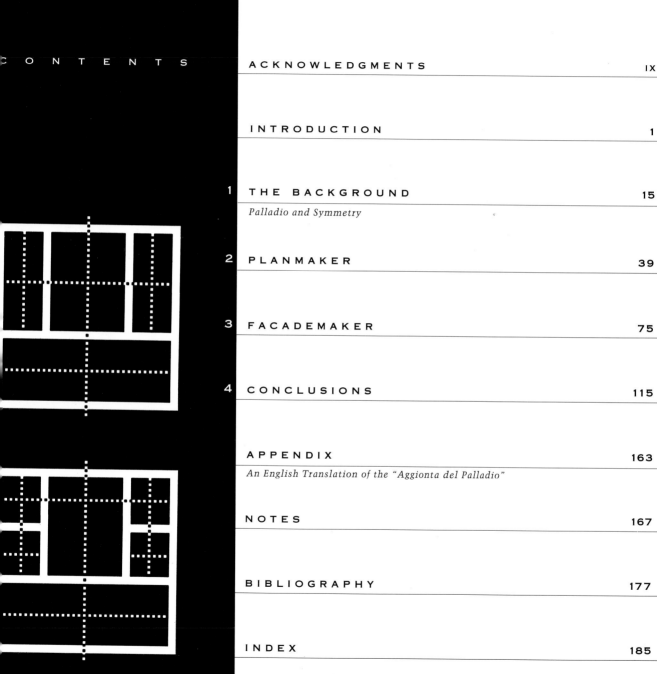

ACKNOWLEDGMENTS

The authors would like to thank Roger Conover, Robert Frew, Claude Palisca, Victor Bers, Rachel Adar, Robert Jan van Pelt, James Ackerman, Donald Hersey, John Davies, Irving Lavin, Thomas Seebohm, Thomas Schumaker, Carroll William Westfall, and Gordon Williams, as well as the four anonymous readers of the manuscript for the MIT Press, and our copyeditor, Matthew Abbate, all of whom made fruitful suggestions for improvement.

INTRODUCTION

Palladio is sometimes called the most influential architect in history. The Palladian and the neo-Palladian villa, in particular, have dominated important stretches of architectural development from the Renaissance to the present. Certainly no other house designer has enjoyed such prestige and attracted so many direct imitators over so long a period. Many an architect who has built more imposing masterpieces than Palladio's has been less notable in these latter respects. Today, more books and articles than ever are devoted to Palladio.

It is often observed that Palladio's villas embody geometrical rules.[1] But there is less certainty as to precisely what the rules are. He wrote some of them down and hinted at others, but most have to be extrapolated from his work; and that is where the disagreements lie. Even assuming that agreement may one day be reached as to the nature of these rules, it could still be objected that in searching them out we have devalued the originality and genius of this architecture, that we have reduced Palladio to a game. And we do confess, certainly, that we have not attempted here to evaluate the man's genius—though of course we completely acknowledge it.

Anyway, much art *is* gamelike. Numerical analyses, counting, statistics, and the like often accompany artistic greatness. Homer, for example, is a poet with a strong sense of numerical and geometric design. This has been proved by any number of statistical and arithmetical "counts," counts that involve symmetries within speeches, incidents, or plots in which the poet uses a device called "ring-composition,"[2] and in meters and even word order. Sometimes Homer exercises these numerical constraints in an extraordinarily detailed and consistent way, though it is usually something the ordinary reader never notices. Thus Eugene O'Neill, Jr., shows that a word ending in a single short syllable is almost always avoided at position $7\frac{1}{2}$ in Homer's hexameters and that, in the ninth position in the line, with many possibilities to choose from, his word endings are almost completely limited to either short-long-long-long, or short-long-short-short-long.[3] Consciously or unconsciously, Homer obeyed certain numerical rules. He counted, calculated, measured, and mirrored just as so many great artists have done in so many fields. Palladio did the same.

Despite his partial silence on the subject, Palladio does seem to invite us to dig his rules out. By the very fact of publishing the *Quattro Libri dell'Architettura* (1570), with its plans, elevations, and details of ornament—parts of buildings, whole buildings, and procedures for assembling given parts into new wholes—he presupposes a reader who might want to create his own personal selection from the elements provided. In other words the book itself *is* a set of rules, a set of possible plans, possible facades, possible details; rules, or possibilities, that are applied rather than articulated. So in the following pages we are simply taking up Palladio's implicit challenge. Stationing ourselves historically in the late 1560s when, toward the end of his long and splendid career, the architect was readying his book for publication, we watch him play (or replay) forty-odd matches of his architectural game.[4] Then we guess the game's rules.

TWO SCHOOLS OF ANALYSIS

One popular hypothesis that seems relevant to our project is that the geometrical rules governing Palladio's plans and facades are assemblages of "ideal" shapes, or that "ideal" or "harmonic" dimensions are used.[5] This of course reflects the common Renaissance idea that certain numbers and shapes are nobler than others. A 4:3 rectangle is superior, say, to a 46:39 rectangle because it is a simpler, more basic proportion to calculate. (Four divided by three is $1\frac{1}{3}$, 46 divided by 39 is 1.179487195; the relatively commensurable $1\frac{1}{3}$ was greatly preferred to 1.179487195, which for practical purposes is incommensurable.) The 4:3 rectangle was also thought to be more harmonious, more beautiful, than rectangles of the latter type. These ideal shapes have been a field of architectural study ever since Rudolf Wittkower published his classic *Architectural Principles in the Age of Humanism*, which first appeared during World War II.[6] Robert Streitz, Colin Rowe, and D. H. Feinstein are among the many authors who have followed in Wittkower's footsteps.

On a quite different tack, G. Stiny, W. J. Mitchell, and others have shown how Palladian plans can be generated by a "parametric generative grammar," or shape grammar, named by analogy to the linguistic work of Noam Chomsky.[7] Their work is exceedingly novel but the basic idea is an old one. The notion that a recipe or algorithm can generate plans, facades, and designs for entire buildings goes back at least to the Roman architectural writer Vitruvius, who was the undisputed god of Renaissance architecture.[8] As Stiny and L. March further point out, the idea was taken up in the Renaissance by Leone Battista Alberti and Leonardo and developed later on by such diverse figures as Goethe, Monge, Froebel, Frege, and Wittgenstein.[9] But now the shape grammarians carry the idea further by developing a set of algebraic "productions," or transformations, that can analyze Palladio's plans into discrete rules. It is curious that the two groups, those who study proportions and those who study shape grammars, seem so little aware of each other's work.

Among the Wittkowerians, Deborah Howard and Malcolm Longair have sought to show that Palladio preferred room dimensions reflecting the ratios of the pitch intervals used in musical scales, especially the major fifth (C–G; ratio 2:3, i.e., the lower note, C, vibrates twice to every three vibrations of the upper note, G) and the perfect fourth (C–F; 3:4).[10] (The idea makes etymological sense, after all, since the Latin word *intervallum* means "between the walls.") Howard and Longair print a list of 34 preferred dimensions using Palladio's Vicentine foot of 34.7 centimeters. The dimensions range between 1 and 100 and are produced by dividing one musical ratio into another. The authors show that Palladio used these preferred dimensions 65–70 percent of the time; had he chosen at random they would have appeared only 45 percent of the time.[11] Hence he really did seem to think that certain lengths and widths were preferable to others, though not exclusively so.

But as the authors themselves point out, many of these same ratios could equally well have come from the purely visual proportions advocated by Vitruvius (*De architectura libri decem* 6.3).[12] There is no real necessity to assume that they were chosen *because* they were musical. Vitruvius himself says not a word about deriving architectural proportions from musical intervals, despite the fact that some of his proportions do coincide with the musical ones, and though he does talk about musical intervals elsewhere in his book (e.g., *De architectura* 5.4). More significantly, perhaps, Palladio, in his own discussion of villa designs (Book II of his *Quattro Libri*), also makes no mention of musical intervals as a source for proportions. No more does his colleague, fellow theorist, collaborator, and patron, Daniele Barbaro, in his annotated edition of Vitruvius—and this despite the fact that he had a strong interest both in proportions and in music.[13]

Finally, Howard and Longair omit a crucial fact, namely that only four of their eight musical intervals were considered consonant in Renaissance harmony. The others were classified as dissonant, to be avoided except as necessary ways of getting from one consonance to another. The consonances were normally C–C (1:1, the unison), C–F (3:4, the fourth, also known as the diatessaron), C–G (2:3, the fifth or diapente), and C–C' (1:2, the octave or diapason). More problematic were the thirds and sixths. Today these intervals are considered consonant, but in the Renaissance they were tuned in myriad ways and could sound extremely harsh. The ratios Howard and Longair cite for the major third (C–E, 64:81) and the major sixth (C–A, 16:27), though used, had no particularly privileged status. The other ratios for thirds and sixths that were commonly accepted in the Renaissance, if all incorporated in the Howard and Longair scheme, would have greatly lengthened their list of acceptable ratios. On the other hand, these authors also give ratios that were, in music, definitely to be avoided as harmonies. These are the major second (C–D, 8:9) and the major seventh (C–B, 128:243). In a recent article that supplements the Howard and Longair findings, Branko Mitrovic has added the hopelessly dissonant augmented fourth (C–F#), which is based on the ratio of 1 to the square root of 2.[14]

It is true that all these proportions, even the last, might well appear in architecture. But an architect could hardly have chosen a good many of them on the grounds that they embodied the ideal qualities of music. Why would he want the visual equivalent of dissonance?[15] These intervals are present in architecture despite, not because of, their role in Renaissance music. Yet Howard and Longair, and Mitrovic, never question their assumption that all musical ratios were uniformly desirable.[16]

The argument that architectural proportions were *derived* from musical ones, then, is hard to sustain. Yet we have noted that many musical proportions are indeed simultaneously architectural. And it is also true that Palladio and Barbaro, for example, thought in terms of a narrow canon of *visual* ratios just as the musicians had a canon of musical ones. More than once Palladio, for instance, says that most rooms in a house should have plans that are square, or else should be rectangles equal to $1\frac{1}{3}$, $1\frac{1}{2}$, or $1\frac{2}{3}$ squares, or at most two squares.[17] These fractions work out to the following set of rectangles (with the addition of a $1:\sqrt{2}$ or root-2 rectangle, which he also recommends):

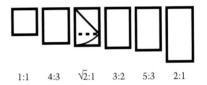

| 1:1 | 4:3 | √2̄:1 | 3:2 | 5:3 | 2:1 |

Let us note immediately that four of the six ratios are musical—and consonant. They correspond to the unison (1:1), fourth (3:4), fifth (2:3), and octave (1:2).[18] Even the root-2 rectangle (the fearful augmented fourth), which is technically incommensurable, could be rather brusquely rounded off to 2:3 or 3:4.[19]

Yet Palladio also uses shapes, sometimes even for principal rooms, that are not on this list. Indeed, according to Howard and Longair, he uses his own recommended canon for only 39 percent of his principal rooms.[20] For example, the 7:8 rectangle (an acceptable musical interval, by the way, only in the highly theoretical Ptolemaic scale) frequently appears. The main *salone* of the Palazzo Antonini in Udine, 32 × 28, has this shape (fig. 4.32).[21] One very practical reason for breaking with the canon (as we have discovered by doing the research for this book) is that it is often geometrically impossible, using lines or walls of the conventional thicknesses found in Palladio's printed plans, to split a given rectangle into smaller ones while at the same time sticking to the canonical proportions and never having any space left over.[22]

The students of proportion rarely tackle the problem of architectural distribution: a given villa's actual layout and sequence of rooms. Those who work on shape grammars, on the other hand, have concentrated on distribution to the exclusion of proportions and even dimensions.[23] And this indeed may be the more promising track to follow. The shape grammarians, furthermore, have been concerned not simply with analyzing but with *generating* Palladian plans—a thing "harmonic" analysis could never do. And they have produced at least two that to us are convincingly Palladian.[24] They do not tell us whether their grammar created these published plans unaided or whether it was coaxed along for the occasion; whether they chose two convincing plans out of a welter of unconvincing ones or whether the shape grammar produced Palladian plans only, or mainly. (That is a question we ourselves will be dealing with.) However, by removing the question of proportion for a later inquiry (not yet undertaken), the grammarians acknowledge the importance of proportion and tacitly endorse the prevailing view that canonical and musical proportions are a critical component of Palladio's villa plan style. We will probe this view in chapter 4.

The drawback of the grammar-generated plans up to the present is that all are formed of squares or integral multiples thereof. The results range from the possibly Palladian (*a*) to a pure un-Palladian and unarchitectural grid (*b*):

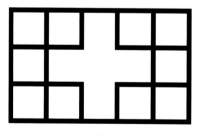

a

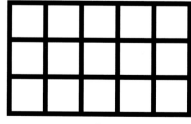

b

What the authors mean is not that Palladio or anyone else would design such a house as the latter, but that this 5 × 3 grid has parameters that can be internally altered but not exceeded. It is a limiting case. Yet plans formed from squares and their multiples can never be truly Palladian. They omit all the intermediate room shapes listed above, formed from squares plus fractions of squares, which comprise Palladio's *only* specifically expressed rule on the subject.[25] Nor do we learn, via the shape grammar as currently developed, anything about the *frequency* with which Palladio employed a given shape; nor does the grammar, so far, generate facades—though this could probably be done fairly easily.

PARADIGMATIC DESIGN

It is the purpose of this book to push further the possibilities of all this promising, important, but incomplete earlier work. We will utilize a simple method of plan and facade design adapting a technique Palladio himself uses and describes. We will then propose a set of rules that not only produce Palladian designs but prevent, or at least downplay, non-Palladian ones.

We have said that Palladio is called the most influential architect who ever lived. One reason for this influence, we believe, is that his villa designs can be replicated with set variations such as we will be describing in this book. In a sense what we have done is simply to make explicit what earlier neo-Palladians have done by instinct. History is full of building types that can be similarly treated. One has only to think of Greek Doric temples, or Hindu temples, or Île-de-France Gothic cathedrals—or, for that matter, Cape Cod cottages. The Greek temples, for example, are all, or almost all, rectangular with perimeters marked by one or two rows of columns and an inner chambered compartment. There are formula-based limitations on length and width, on the number and shape of columns, and on everything to do with ornamental detail.

But the strict paradigms and limited variants of these temples and cathedrals have not resulted from a single architect's having reasoned out a basic idea and then run it through a series of permutations. Instead, in these earlier sets of variations one architect simply borrowed a scheme from another, or from several others, and then created a new variation on it. This can result in a pool of "possible" temples or cathedrals—or possible Cape Cod cottages—comparable to the pool of possible villas we will be looking at. But Palladio's pool is different from most of these others because it is the work of a single person.

This, in turn, means several things. Palladio's name belongs with the concept of the Palladian villa in a way quite different from that in which, say, the name of Konrad Roriczer, architect of the cathedral at Regensburg, is associated with the cathedral type to which that building belongs. It would be hard to prove (though not inconceivable) that Roriczer wanted to spell out a range of variations on his chosen theme. But, for whatever reason, he did not do so. The early Renaissance architects Filarete and Francesco di Giorgio come closer to Palladio in this respect, but they provide only a few instances of each type and let it go at that. One *could* consider their meager collections "pools" and extrapolate rules from them. But any such rules would probably be incomplete and awry. Leonardo, we shall see, was more interested than his predecessors in rule-based architectural variations. But Palladio is the first great architect in European history to work out *many* variations on a basic theme, and to build a considerable number of them as separate structures. (His contemporary Sebastiano Serlio published a book roughly comparable to the *Quattro Libri* in its intention, but he could not be called a "great" architect.)[26]

Palladio and Serlio, furthermore, actually print their specimen designs in quantities sufficient for us to start speaking of rules and, almost more important, statistical frequencies. For these reasons Palladio is the predecessor of a host of later paradigm-minded architects running from Claude-Nicolas Ledoux (the Paris customhouses) to Le Corbusier (the villas) to Frank Lloyd Wright (the prairie houses). He also anticipates, at a much higher level of achievement, the innumerable essays in prefabrication, modular kits, model housing, etc., that began to appear in the eighteenth century and have since then only grown more numerous and varied.

Let us call this kind of architecture paradigmatic. Paradigmatic architecture generates buildings according to rules expressed by a model in the same way that large numbers of Latin verbs obey the paradigm of *amo, amas, amat* as it moves through all the endings, tenses, moods, and inner transformations that a Latin verb may have. And not only does the paradigm of *amo* apply to hundreds, maybe thousands of existing Latin verbs, one could in fact generate new verbs with it. In other words, following the lead of George Stiny, W. J. Mitchell, and others, we are applying the essential notion of a generative grammar to the history and analysis of architecture.[27]

What led Palladio to take up paradigmatic design? Obviously one factor was that he was faced with many similar programs for similar clients (a large clientele of gentlemen farmers who wanted beautiful villas on their estates). But there were other factors. We will be noting the sheer novelty of symmetry (in its modern sense) in Palladio's day and will show what great use he made of it. May not one half of a symmetrical building be said to have "generated" the other? Could this in fact not reinforce the idea of an architecture of set variations? And of course Palladio's book itself was one more in a recently begun paradigmatic series of architectural treatises for which Vitruvius provided the *amo, amas, amat*. Francesco di Giorgio and Serlio, in particular, had just written books with specimen plans, specimen doorways, specimen windows, specimen columns, and the like. Their approach, like Palladio's, seems to say: "Conjugate these forms by yourself in accordance with the rules stated here." It is no coincidence, by the way, that two of the great ages of architectural treatise-writing were two of the great ages of paradigmatic design—ancient Greece with its temples (unfortunately the Greek treatises are lost, but Vitruvius mentions sixty or so), and Renaissance Italy.

One good way of divining the existence of a rule is to watch what happens when it is broken. Our method will be to create villa plans and facades based on Palladio's ideas; but our designs will lead us gradually from his more obvious rules to his less obvious ones. As we continue the process, each time we make a mistake we will identify and correct it. Eventually we will produce plans and facades that, in our opinion at least, get really close to what Palladio himself would do. We do not do this in order to build new Palladian villas, though that is a perfectly reasonable possibility. Rather, knowing what Palladio would and would not do deepens our understanding of what he actually did do.

THE USE OF THE COMPUTER

We have decided to teach a computer to design Palladian villas rather than doing it ourselves with pencil and paper. At this point we should repeat that, notwithstanding our reliance on a computer, the method we use is itself one that Palladio advocated. There is nothing ahistorical about it. What the computer contributes is simply the ability to calculate a huge number of possible permutations and combinations based on Palladio's rules. Because of the rapidity and completeness with which it can apply these rules, it can test them on a far wider and firmer basis than could an unaided human being. With the disk containing Planmaker and Facademaker, our software for creating plans and facades, anyone can sit down in front of a Macintosh and generate thousands of Palladian villas. The ultimate number is probably circumscribed only by the operator's patience. We had thought of calling this book *All Possible Palladian Villas*, but it has been pointed out to us that the random number generator that stands at the core of our system has limitations. It is not true that even our thousands actually represent *all* the possibilities.

But without the computer, furthermore, it would be harder to learn from our mistakes. Since we define what Palladio did by discovering what he would not do, we must discover *everything* he would not do. That is another reason for the phrase "possible villas." True, our data consist of the 44 villa and house designs in Book II of the *Quattro Libri*—not a large set of models. Indeed even some of these 44 have been ruled out for reasons that will be discussed. Yet if one multiplies 44 by every possible application of each of our rules, the result is astronomical. Once again, only the computer can ring all the changes. Only the computer can prove that a rule, even if followed in every possible way, will still yield the proper results.

The computer has yet another advantage: it excludes unconscious human prejudice. It eliminates the personality of Palladio's modern student and concentrates exclusively on the 44 designs. We will see in chapter 4 that certain architects who thought of themselves as imitators of Palladio, for example Lord Burlington, could stray very far from his architectural code. Burlington, who lived two centuries after his idol, translated Palladio's house plans very much into his own terms. We don't know whether this was conscious or unconscious. Either way, the computer lacks Burlington's unacknowledged prejudices. It has no idea what we want it to do; it merely does what we tell it to do. That is the crucial point. It makes every rule explicit and unambiguous.

There are still other advantages in our approach. For one thing, people examine and compare much more carefully when they have before them both an authentic work and a good imitation. The imitation teaches us things about the original that no amount of study of the original alone could do. And with Palladio, there are many such things to be learned. Thus it is not simply a question of rules, even subtle ones, that are *always* observed. There are things Palladio always does, things he does only in certain specific circumstances, and things he does sporadically—just for the hell of it. The observations we are about to make, then, write a code for the stylistic analysis of plans and facades, a code that consists partly of unbreakable rules and partly of mere tendencies. Statistics establish just how strong or weak a given tendency is.

Our new technique, we hope, will also help create new ways, useful both for the historian and the practitioner, of doing architectural history. Not only can our system be used to judge the precise degree of Palladianism in the work of Burlington and his school, or, say, in that of Palladians in the United States; it can be extended to paradigmatic architecture that has nothing to do with Palladio, and there, presumably, allow equally new insights.

But what will these new insights be? Will we really have made a contribution to architectural history, to understanding a great architect's mind, or will we simply have produced a video game for architecturally minded grown-ups? Let us answer that with a second linguistic analogy: many highly intelligent people, some of them, indeed, great writers, learn languages, and speak and write them flawlessly, without being able to articulate the grammatical rules that structure those languages. Good writers know right from wrong simply on the basis of the way the words sound. Such people may be able to state certain basic rules, e.g., that a verb has to agree in number with its subject, but they may well never have heard of the frequentative imperfect, that bane of nonnative English speakers.[28] Yet good writers and speakers know instinctively when this tense should and should not be employed. It is the same with Palladio. He may have articulated only some of his rules—he might even have been *unable* to articulate others—but they are nonetheless there, and he obeyed them.

The advantage of articulating these immanent rules is that they etch out, with hitherto unexperienced clarity, the procedures and habits that distinguish this great architect from all others. Knowing them makes it immediately possible to distinguish, in a quantifiable and unquestionable way, the work of imitators like Scamozzi, or Lord Burlington, or Thomas Jefferson, from Palladio's authentic work. It removes architectural connoisseurship from the realm of instinct and sets it within that of the verifiable. By articulating the rules we newly define and clarify a great man's individuality. In the end we shall find that Palladio's rules, expressed and unexpressed, are as elegant as any geometric proof or algorithm. By showing this, by showing to what extent he was a natural geometer, we do not make him less the great architect; on the contrary, we show, in a way that gives more than mere lip service to the proposition, how great architecture may flow from geometry.

THE BACKGROUND

Palladio and Symmetry

1

One little-discussed aspect of Renaissance geometry clearly fascinated Palladio. As is often observed, all of his villa plans are laid out along a central vertical axis.[1] This axis, in turn, is lined with concentric sequences or strings of spaces. On either side of these central strings the rest of the villa is constructed from room arrangements that strictly reflect each other across the central axis.

Symmetry of this sort is one of the neglected corners of architectural history. Nor is it the simple thing it is sometimes thought to be. Palladio, furthermore, employed it with a subtlety that is beyond that of his contemporaries.[2] Palladio, indeed, came on the scene when the very word "symmetry" meant something different from what it means today. He was part of a movement that deprived the word of this earlier meaning and gave it its modern one. In the course of that shift, symmetry turned from a kind of measurement, and an aesthetic judgment, into a geometric technique.[3] In our own time symmetry has gone on to become a branch of mathematics.

The complexities and pitfalls of symmetry were intriguing to Renaissance architects. Their study of the subject had parallels, and a possible indebtedness, to earlier postclassical art—Byzantine, medieval, and particularly Islamic. The exquisite geometries of the Timurid architecture of Iran and Turan are just one of many cases in point.[4] During the Italian Renaissance, the ringleaders of the symmetry revolution were Alberti, Francesco di Giorgio, Leonardo, Bramante, and Cesare Cesariano, who seem to have been acquainted with one another's work in the early decades of the sixteenth century in Milan.[5]

To the ancients the word "symmetry" meant what its components *syn*, "with," and *metria*, "measurement," would imply: commensuration—two things of the same size and, by extension, two or more integrated measurement systems. By further extension, in this original definition "symmetry" could mean suitable measurement, or proportion—hence beauty. For us this older meaning has been almost completely crowded out by the newer. Thus on remarking that two beams are each 6 feet long we would never say that they were for this reason "symmetrical." Nor would we say that 6 feet is "symmetrical" with 72 inches because we use a system of measurement that has 12 inches per foot and 12 × 6 = 72 (this is what we call commensurability). But Vitruvius does exactly this: he says the "symmetries" of the Corinthian column base and shaft are the same as those of the Ionic (4.1.1), meaning that both have the same proportions and hence are the same number of diameters high. When "symmetry" came to mean what it means today, the word's ancient association with "beautiful" probably strengthened the idea that a design with two identical halves was more beautiful than one without.

It is interesting to watch the ancients describing what we call mirror symmetry; for of course they had the thing itself even if they did not call it by that name. Theophrastus in his *History of the Plants* describes the beauty of foliage leaves (3.18.7; 3.12.9) using the phrase ἔυρυθμα φύλλα, "eurhythmic leaves," drawing on the sense of repetition we still feel in the word "rhythm." But no dictionary of ancient Greek or Latin gives that word the meaning we give it nowadays.

As to the earliest example of "symmetry" in its modern sense, Walter Kambartel notes that when Bernini came to France in 1665 he criticized the Church of the Val-de-Grâce in Paris because one transept was of a very different design from the other. According to Chantelou, who was on the spot and wrote down the great man's words, Bernini used the term *défaut de symétrie*.[6] Eighteen years later Claude Perrault spoke of "our symmetry" (as opposed to the ancient sort) as the *rapport d'égalité*. But, Kambartel *contra*, Perrault never clearly states that "our symmetry" meant bilateral reflection across a central axis.[7] In later books Perrault claims that symmetry means equal size, distribution, and spacing; but here again we do not really have the concept of mirror symmetry in so many words. Aside from Bernini's phrase, we have not found any instances where the word is unambiguously employed in its modern meaning before the nineteenth century. Kambartel cites Charles Blanc's *Grammaire des arts du dessin* (1867), and the *Oxford English Dictionary* provides an instance of about the same date.[8]

Bilateral

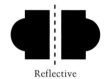

Reflective

Translatory or Glide

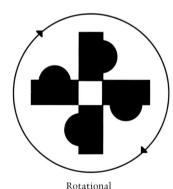

Rotational

1.1 Four basic types of Renaissance symmetry.

It is true that symmetry, in our modern sense, has always existed in nature and art, and not just in leaves. The ancients had of course observed that in a human face, a mammal's body, and dozens of other things in nature, the left half was the mirror of the right. And ancient architects had built temples, baths, and ships that, almost more often than not, were elaborately symmetrical, precisely in the modern sense of the word. But in Western Europe, as far as we can tell, symmetry began to flourish as a geometric discipline, and indeed at times as an architectural necessity, only with the Renaissance. So the following pages on Renaissance symmetry will be discussing a science that was beginning to exist but had not yet gotten itself baptized.

Today, symmetry is usually analyzed in terms of the main types illustrated in figure 1.1. Note that bilateral symmetry is not necessarily the same as reflective (the two upper diagrams). Bilateral symmetry consists simply of two (and not more) similar shapes on an axis. In reflective symmetry the shapes have to be mirror images of each other. There can, furthermore, be multilateral symmetry that is not necessarily reflective and reflective symmetry that involves more than one axis. Translatory or glide symmetry repeats a form axially. As to rotational symmetry, note that another way of saying that a form is rotated is to say that it changes direction, as from north to east. The change of direction is the more marked when the form is compound, when it has a strong directional axis, and when the number of axes is multiplied. In the latter case the same form now points successively north, northeast, east, and so on. In any actual design several of these types of symmetry may overlap.

In the 1460s Antonio Averlino, who adopted the scholarly sobriquet Filarete,[9] produced a treatise on architecture that remained unpublished at the time but seems to have been known. It is full of symmetrical public buildings, churches, town plans, and the like. Much more unusually, it also calls for symmetry in the plans of private houses. Filarete describes a "palace for a gentleman," for example, which, we learn from a close and patient reading of his verbal description, was to have possessed bilateral mirror symmetry.[10] He begins by describing and dimen-

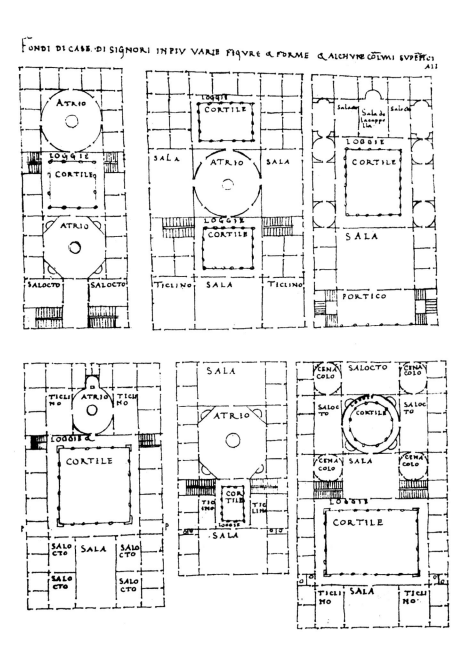

1.2 *Plans from Francesco di Giorgio Martini's* Trattati di architettura, *pl. 199.*

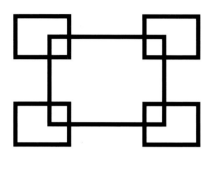

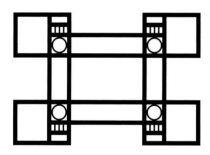

1.3 *Schematic diagram of Poggioreale.*

sioning a central portal, then flanks it left and right with identical strings of rooms that move along the front and down the sides of a central courtyard to form the whole building into a hollow 4:3 rectangle. Unfortunately the illustrators who drew Filarete's plan in surviving manuscripts misread the text and made the house *a*symmetrical. But the attentive reader can have no doubt that Filarete himself is advocating reflective symmetry across the house's vertical axis.[11]

In the 1480s Francesco di Giorgio Martini, a Sienese architect, sculptor, and painter, composed two illustrated architectural treatises, one a corrected and rewritten version of the other. He tells us, erroneously, that what we would call bilateral reflective symmetry ruled house design in antiquity:

The ancients employed several courtyards, some square, some of a square and a third, some of a square and a half, some of two squares, and some oval. Also their elevations were constructed in various ways, so that they were either square or one and a half squares wide; and in distinction to the square courtyards, the oval ones had circular loggias, with vaults and roofs compartmented by their ornament so that all the lines from the center might correspond; and the same thing goes for the square [rectilinear] residence.[12]

Francesco is lavish with illustrations of these rather opaque phrases. Among them he has a few asymmetrical house plans, but the great majority are elaborately symmetrical in the modern sense. What the diagrams tell us is that the central peristyle's columns generate the coordinates of a grid that then shapes the rooms and other spaces grouped around that courtyard (fig. 1.2). The "center" is the courtyard and its columns. The "compartmentation" is the wall grid they generate. The automatic result is that the grid splits the left-hand half of the house into a mirror image of the right.[13]

We can turn now to actual buildings. Particularly crucial, for Palladio, was the villa of Poggioreale, near Naples, erected in the 1480s from a design by Giuliano da Maiano. It was probably the first consciously symmetrical domestic structure of the Renaissance. The first drawing of figure 1.3 shows the plan of the main floor (the upper floor was identical) as a set of overlapping rectangles; in the second

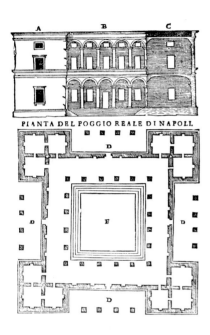

PIANTA DEL POGGIO REALE DI NAPOLI.

1.4 *Serlio's version of Poggioreale,*
from his Tutte l'opere d'architettura e
prospettiva *(1619).*

drawing, these turn into a set of four square towers containing individual living apartments at the corners of an oblong central open court.[14]

Poggioreale, which was destroyed in the eighteenth century, had been erected at the time Francesco di Giorgio was writing his treatises. He had probably seen it; the building was famous in its day and Francesco went several times to Naples in the Neapolitan royal service.[15] Poggioreale's greatest fame, however, came not from those who visited it but from the heavily revamped version of it printed by Sebastiano Serlio, which is what we reproduce (fig. 1.4).[16] Serlio transformed the rectangular plan into a perfect square. This square may be described as being split into seven equal smaller squares per side. The towers are L-shaped clusters of these squares, one cluster at each corner of the large square. Set between the towers are two-story porticoes five arches wide and/or three squares long by one deep. The same module governs the interior portico and stepped central pool.

This arrangement may be thought of as a quintuple vertical split with a ratio of 1:1:3:1:1 crossed by an identical horizontal split (fig. 1.5). This means that, unlike the actual villa, Serlio's version of the building had four identical facades. This version of Poggioreale seems to have been the first such house plan of the Renaissance. In short (as we shall see), the design had both reflective and rotational symmetry.

The impact of Serlio's version of Poggioreale was immense. A whole dissertation has been written about its influence in later domestic architecture, using French examples alone![17] The scheme obviously fascinated Palladio. One of the first buildings to which his main early patron, the poet Giangiorgio Trissino, introduced the budding architect was Trissino's Villa Cricoli.[18] This had been remodeled by Trissino himself so that its main facade resembled that of Poggioreale.

The beauty of Poggioreale, to a generation that was coming to admire the play of symmetry, was that it could be interestingly disassembled and reassembled. To show this, we have concocted a second split diagram that restates the ideas in figure 1.5. In figure 1.6 the L-shaped blocks of Serlio's scheme have arms of equal length and width. The most obvious type of disassembly or splitting here is into

1.5 Serlio's Poggioreale generated by
1:1:3:1:1 splits.

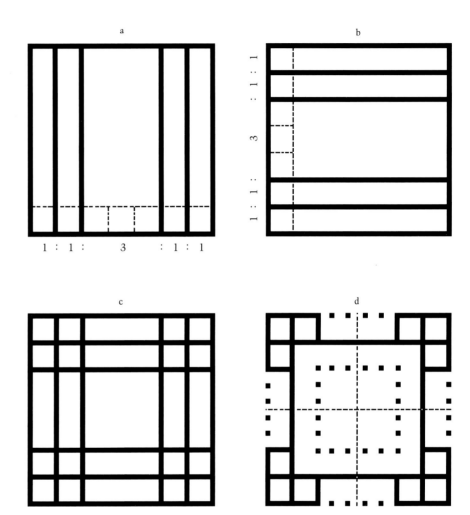

a

1 : 1 :   3   : 1 : 1

b

1 : 1 :   3   : 1 : 1

c

d

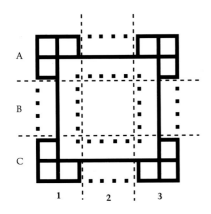

*1.6   Serlio's Poggioreale divided into a
3 × 3 grid of squares.*

three parts (though double, quintuple, and sextuple splits are possible). With three-way horizontal and vertical splits, one gets a wider central axis consisting of the central square peristyle and the upper and lower exterior porticoes. Laterally flanking this axial string of spaces are two fragments that form reflective symmetries. These consist of the L-shaped apartments in the towers, two on each side of the axis. Horizontally, as noted, one gets exactly the same thing rotated 90°. We have noted the horizontal splits as A, B, and C and the vertical ones as 1, 2, and 3. Most of Palladio's plans are based on this general idea, although most of his buildings are also oblong and hence have vertical and horizontal axes of unequal weight.

Serlio's version of Poggioreale, with its four-way identical layout, is, indeed, the geometrical cousin of Palladio's most famous villa, the Rotonda (fig. 1.7d). Once the Serlian villa's basic constituents have been split apart, as here, it is easy to move them around, keeping them on their original axes but sliding them together or apart so as to make new plans. Thus, using the Poggioreale components of three square rooms forming an L-shaped corner (fig. 1.7a), we slide them all toward the center to create a hollow square (fig. 1.7b). The hollow center of this square can otherwise be defined as the square formed by grouping four of the basic room modules together. That inner square can then be multiplied to create four axial porticoes outside the rooms, whose columns are supplied by the four identical original porticoes on the four faces of Serlio's Poggioreale (fig. 1.7c). Finally the central space, still four times the basic module, can be filled with a circle whose diameter is one side of that same square. Making this circle the base of a dome, we would then have converted Serlio's Poggioreale into a respectable version of Palladio's Villa Rotonda.[19] Note that the triple vertical and horizontal splits in our scheme for Poggioreale match those in the scheme for the Rotonda. The type of manipulation we pursue here involves what is known today as glide symmetry.[20]

Among other built structures, one of the earliest house plans that is fully and, seemingly, consciously symmetrical in the modern sense is that of the Strozzi palace in Florence, begun in 1488. The building is generally attributed to Giuliano

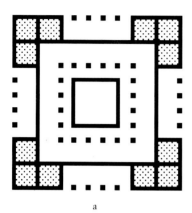

a

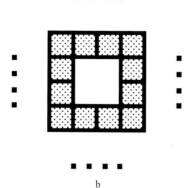

b

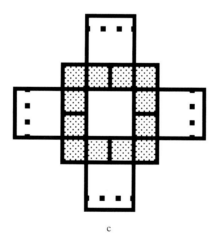

c

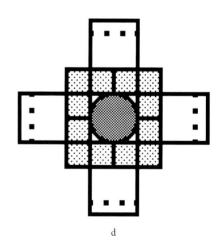

d

*1.7 Transformation of Serlio's Poggioreale
into the Villa Rotonda.*

da Sangallo, Benedetto da Maiano (brother of the architect of Poggioreale), and an architect called Cronaca (fig. 1.8). The Strozzi plan consists, first, of a six-way vertical split whose intervals are designated by the *a* and *b* modules in the diagram. The ratio of the intervals is 5:3:5:5:3:5. There is also a four-way horizontal split whose intervals are all equal to one side of *a*, in other words having the ratio 5:5:5:5. As with Poggioreale, we can disassemble the plan of the Strozzi palace into L-shaped components (fig. 1.9). The four L's are identical in size, shape, and subdivisions; each matches its neighbor when reflected across the vertical or horizontal axis. We show them stacked together (lower right) to prove this. Each is then rotated or reflected around the building's central point in a different way. Thus, for example, if two of the clusters are removed from the stack and flipped or mirrored so as to be turned upside down, one of these can become the building's upper right-hand corner. The other is flipped again, this time crosswise, to become the upper left-hand corner. Finally, one of the two L's remaining in the lower right can also be flipped crosswise, which turns it into the building's lower left-hand corner.

This principle of mirroring and/or rotating identical L-shaped corner clusters became endemic in Renaissance architecture and was often employed by Palladio. Our computer will in effect be doing the same thing, though it does this without needing commands like "flip vertically" and "rotate 90°."

Aside from his obvious fascination with symmetry for its own sake, Palladio also gives a practical reason for it:

The stanze *[i.e., as opposed to the entry hall and* sala *or main hall] should be compartmented on the two sides of the entrance hall and* sala; *and one must warn that those on the right-hand side must correspond to, and be equal to, those on the left. Thus the fabric will be the same on one side as on the other, and the walls will take the weight of the roof equally. For if the* stanze *are large on one side [of the house] and small on the other, these latter will be more apt to resist the weight since the walls will be more frequent, while [the other side] will be weaker. Whence, in time, will come the greatest inconveniences, which will ruin the work.*[21]

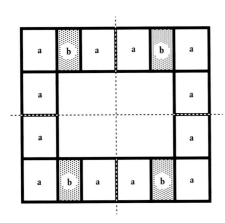

1.8 *Symmetries and proportions in the Strozzi palace.*

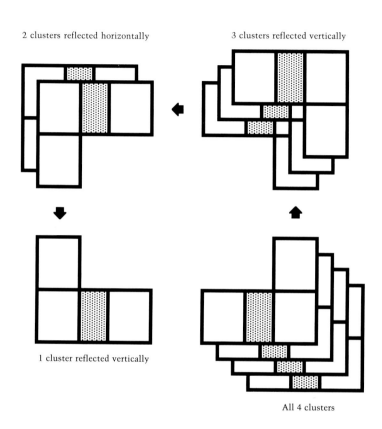

2 clusters reflected horizontally

3 clusters reflected vertically

1 cluster reflected vertically

All 4 clusters

1.9   Generating the Strozzi palace by
reflecting L-shaped room groups.

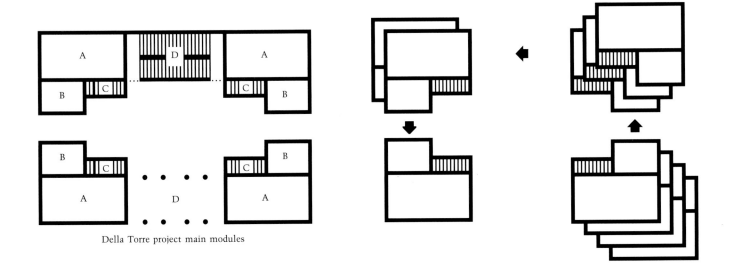

Della Torre project main modules

1.10 *L-shaped room groups in Palladio's Palazzo Della Torre.*

In other words, symmetry is a physical necessity. An asymmetrical house will settle unevenly since one side weighs more than the other. (There is a lot of marshy ground in the Veneto.) A further inspiration, a social one, for symmetrical plans lies in the regional tradition of separate but equal apartments for man and wife, each with its *salone*, dining room, chamber, and other facilities.

In figure 1.10 we see how Palladio builds on the basic idea of L-shaped corner blocks that we saw in Poggioreale and the Strozzi palace. These diagrams have been extrapolated from a design in the *Quattro Libri* for a city house in Verona designed for a family named Della Torre.[22] In the basic layout, four rectangles (marked A) measuring 36 by 20 [Vicentine?] feet,[23] which is reducible to a proportion of roughly 7:4, anchor the corners of the plan. Another shape, 20 by 15 feet (whose width thus equals the height of the 7:4 rectangle), forms a 4:3 rectangle. Four of these are arranged lengthwise, flanking either end of the horizontal or minor axis, at the house's two side entrances (marked B). Four small stairways, whose length equals the difference between the 7:4 and the 4:3 rectangles as here arranged, are tucked into the inner corners where the 7:4 and the 4:3 rectangles join (marked C). (These small rectangles are shaded to show that they are staircases.) The shaded central 2:1 rectangle in the upper row is another, much larger stair. The central lower 2:1 rectangle, in turn, forms the columned entranceway (D) leading to the villa's central courtyard. As with Strozzi, the plan contains four L-shaped building blocks each symmetrical with the others when reflected across the horizontal or vertical axes. Alternatively, one can think of each L being rotated 180°, e.g., from the northeast to the southwest.

Other components of the Della Torre plan can be produced by interlocking and overlapping the component rectangles. To demonstrate this we assemble the 7:4, the 4:3, and the small stair into four L's similar to those in our diagram of the Strozzi. We can now recognize this form as the plan's basic L-shaped building block made out of the individual rectangles. This L-shape becomes the plan's upper right-hand corner, and is then mirrored and/or rotated until the whole layout is achieved.

However when we consider the Della Torre plan simply as the result of such splits, as with Poggioreale, we run into a problem. Some of the lines created by the splitting process will have to be erased because they are not present in the finished product we are attempting to recreate. We shall see in the next chapter that there is a way of making these erasures.

Note that the vertical axes of these plans are not so much imaginary lines as concentric strings or groupings of rooms. A space the width of the 2:1 rectangle creates the vertical axis in the Della Torre plan. The horizontal axis is the width of that vertical axis minus the heights of two 4:3 rectangles. One can imagine the architect working out the plan with a single paper cutout of the L-block divided into its three component rectangles. He would simply trace that cutout into its various positions, as needed, to make the completed house plan.

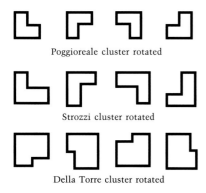

Poggioreale cluster rotated

Strozzi cluster rotated

Della Torre cluster rotated

1.11 *Rotations of L-shapes.*

Looking back at Serlio's Poggioreale (fig. 1.5) and comparing it with the Strozzi (fig. 1.8) and Della Torre plans (fig. 1.10), we see what might be considered two different branches of rotational/reflective symmetry (fig. 1.11). When Poggioreale's L, which has arms of equal length and width, is rotated into new positions, with each new location its arms go off in two new directions—first up and right, then down and right, then down and left, and finally up and left. But the arms of the Strozzi and Della Torre L's are unequal. Therefore, when rotated or reflected, the longer arm always sets up a new *main* direction: right, down, left, up. The Poggioreale type of L is usable in central-plan buildings like the Rotonda—or for that matter Bramante's project for St. Peter's. The Strozzi type is useful in buildings with unequal axes such as most of Palladio's villas—and indeed most Renaissance palaces.

The diagram in figure 1.12 illustrates twelve types of symmetry that are achievable with L-shaped blocks in which one arm is longer than the other. In each case the black L is the original block, the white L the one that has been altered. Once the possibilities for two L's are established, one can proceed to work with larger numbers of L's (the bottom row in fig. 1.12). One could then investigate the possibilities of L's in which not only the length of the arms varied but also their thickness.

The medieval villa tradition of the Veneto, where most of Palladio's houses were built, knew nothing of all this. One does find the simplest forms of translatory and bilateral symmetry here and there. But such plans are of the most rudimentary type—four identically shaped rooms in a row, for example. The other traditional types of villa or farmhouse plans in the region were asymmetrical, as Martin Kubelik has shown.[24] Therefore, in designing his own villas, Palladio was probably less interested in this local vernacular than in the advanced architectural games of people like Francesco di Giorgio and Giuliano da Maiano.

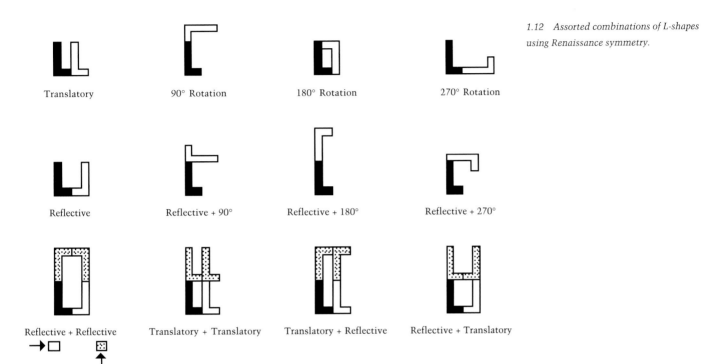

Translatory   90° Rotation   180° Rotation   270° Rotation

Reflective   Reflective + 90°   Reflective + 180°   Reflective + 270°

Reflective + Reflective   Translatory + Translatory   Translatory + Reflective   Reflective + Translatory

1.12   *Assorted combinations of L-shapes using Renaissance symmetry.*

The great pioneer in rotational symmetry was Leonardo da Vinci. He should be mentioned at this point, therefore, but at the same time it should be noted that his work on symmetry was less relevant to Palladio than were such models as Poggioreale and the Strozzi palace. Leonardo's small sketches of church plans have become famous.[25] Like Palladio's villas, Leonardo's drawings of central-plan churches are fundamental constituents of High Renaissance and later architecture.[26] But we shall see that they are, as well, simply ecclesiastical variants of the Poggioreale principle.

Most of Leonardo's church plans involve small chapels—squares, hemispheres, and cylinders—clustering around a main central space. The churches are like planets with multiple identical moons. Sometimes the "planet" is simply a jumbo version of the "moons," sometimes not (fig. 1.13). In the left-hand diagram, which is adapted from one of Leonardo's sketches, we see an octagonal *cappella maggiore* around which an axis is rotated into eight positions, moving 45° each time. The "moon" that is rotated is a small square chapel with three apses. Note that, since the moon is in itself asymmetrical on one of its axes, its direction changes markedly every time it moves. The final church is a kind of compass rose, with a north chapel, a northeast chapel, an east chapel, and so on. The same kinds of rotation occurred with the house plans we looked at earlier. But with the Strozzi/ Della Torre type there was reflection as well as rotation. With Poggioreale itself the sense of a rotation is less obvious because there are fewer instances of it. With Leonardo's schemes, rotation becomes the most prominent feature.

In the right-hand design in figure 1.13, also adapted from Leonardo, we see the same arrangement except that at north, east, south, and west the chapels are cylindrical. Thus Leonardo not only experimented with rotational symmetry of this strongly directional type, he could deploy his components in alternating repetitions. Within these repetitions, in turn, axiality could alternate with nonaxiality, direction with nondirection. In both cases, however, and in all his other central-plan designs, Leonardo simply adds intermediate compass points to the basic north, east, south, west of the Poggioreale principle.

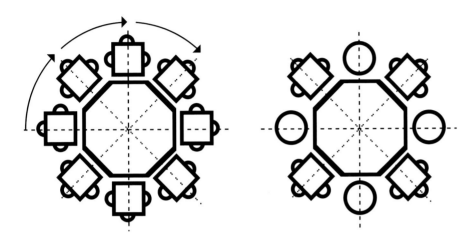

1.13 *Rotational symmetry in one of Leonardo's church perspectives. After Ms. B, 5v, Bibliothèque Nationale, Paris.*

STRONGLY MISREADING VITRUVIUS

Filarete, Francesco di Giorgio, and the designers of the Strozzi palace and Poggioreale all belong to the fifteenth century. They knew about Vitruvius though they probably did not have an intimate and correct knowledge of his text. And even Leonardo, who lived well into the sixteenth century, had left Italy by the time the Roman author was being seriously studied in print, translated into Italian, and illustrated. The first printed Vitruvius is 1511, in Latin, and the first Italian translations (which remained in manuscript), were done some time in the following decade. Important annotated and illustrated editions appeared in 1521, 1556, and 1567.

With Vitruvius now so well established on the architectural scene, people became anxious to link him to the vogue for the new, de facto but unnamed fad for what we call symmetry. For these purposes Vitruvius's passages on house design, while not unhelpful, required vigorous reinterpretation. Vitruvius never specifically calls for symmetrical house plans and facades. His prescriptions for what we know as symmetry are limited to public buildings, especially temples. In fact the Greek and Roman houses Vitruvius would have known were almost always

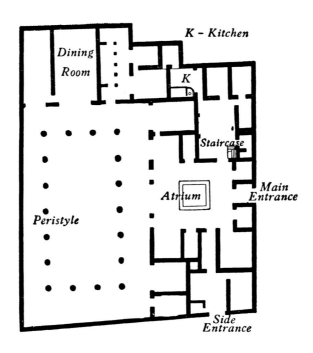

1.14 Domus Vettiorum, Pompeii, plan.
From Vitruvius's Ten Books of Architecture, *volume II, edited and translated by*
Frank Granger (Cambridge, Mass., 1934);
reprinted by permission of Harvard University Press and The Loeb Classical Library.

asymmetrical.[27] The Domus Vettiorum, Pompeii (fig. 1.14), shows the characteristic look of these ancient layouts.[28] It is true, on the other hand, that, very occasionally, ancient houses *were* perfectly symmetrical. The so-called Casa della Farnesina in Rome, under the site of the present Villa Farnesina on the Tiber, is a case in point. But this structure was not known in the sixteenth century.[29]

Nonetheless Palladio and his predecessors made elaborate plans that endowed ancient villas and palaces with intricate plays of reflective, translatory, and other kinds of symmetry. But these drawings were really *jeux d'esprit* rather than serious restorations. In Palladio's time the best way of achieving classical authority for the kind of symmetry we have been looking at was to discover it in Vitruvius—whether it was there or not.[30] There are two places where Vitruvius verges on the idea that a house should be symmetrical. Speaking of house plans (6.2.1), he says: "The architect's greatest concern is that the system governing the compartments within his buildings should be in proportion to a fixed module [*rata pars*]." But a house need not be symmetrical in order to be modular.

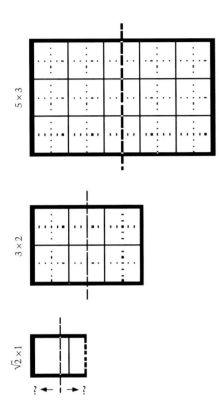

5 × 3

3 × 2

√2 × 1

? ← | → ?

1.15 Vitruvius's canonical proportions for an atrium.

Vitruvius's subsequent discussions of domestic architecture, furthermore, fully allow for asymmetrical plans and elevations such as those of the House of the Vettii. The second point at which Vitruvius verges on a call for symmetry in domestic architecture is when he describes the atrium, which in the Roman house is a kind of antechamber to the main courtyard. Here he gives the proper length and width. There are in fact three options: the 3:2, the 5:3, and the √2:1 rectangles. Only the first two of these, of course, involve implicit modules (fig. 1.15). Vitruvius also prescribes height ratios for each of the three floor plans, and adds proportions for peristyles (4:3), triclinia (2:1), and exedrae (apselike niches, 1:1). Let us note that while symmetrical splitting is of course possible with a √2:1 rectangle, using rectangular modules rather than square ones, the kind of subdivisions we see in Palladio are really only practicable with square modules and hence with rectangles such as 4:3, 5:3, etc.[31]

But what Vitruvius in his text fails to say could be said for him by his annotators. In 1521 Cesare Cesariano, a Milanese architect and pupil of Bramante, produced a generously annotated and illustrated edition of Vitruvius's text.[32] He took it upon himself also to correct, or shall we say clarify and extend, Vitruvius's prescriptions for domestic architecture. Cesare forces his author to champion symmetrical house plans in two places—once where Vitruvius talks about temples (3.1ff.) and once where he talks about houses (6.4ff.).

Book 3, chapter 1 of Vitruvius contains all sorts of geometrical rules about temple design. In his commentary, Cesare insists that here Vitruvius means to apply these rules to houses as well as to temples. (He even says they should apply to entire cities.) For, Cesare explains, when Vitruvius uses the word *aedes* to refer to temples, we are to recall that *aedes* can in fact mean any sort of building, including houses.[33] What, he asks, are temples anyway but the *houses* of the gods? When, slightly later, Vitruvius is again writing of temples, Cesare again amends the text: "that is, temples *and the houses* [for the temple staff] built around them."[34]

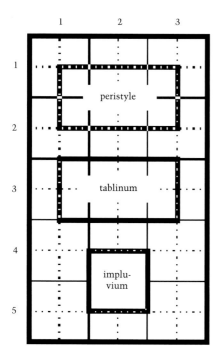

1.16 *Proportions of Cesariano's Roman house plan. After Cesare Cesariano,* Di Lucio Vitruvio Pollione de architectura libri dece *(Como, 1521).*

When Vitruvius actually does start speaking about house plans, Cesare gets another chance to fortify his case. Where Vitruvius, as we have just seen, provides rules for a limited number of spaces but with no specified overall relationship, Cesare says that a proper house plan *has* to be symmetrical, in our modern sense, though of course he doesn't use the term. How does he get away with putting these words in Vitruvius's mouth? By yet more radical emendation. When Vitruvius starts talking about atria (6.3.3), Cesare claims that the word atrium means not only the atrium proper but the whole building. "For Ovid in the first book of the *Metamorphoses* says this: *atria nobilium valvis celebrantur apertis,* 'the open-doored atria of the nobles [are filled with] celebrants' " (1.173). As Cesare correctly adds, classical poets by metonymy (taking the part for the whole) often called the whole house the "atrium," usually using the plural, *atria.*[35]

When Vitruvius calls for geometrical atria, in short, he is calling for geometrical houses. Cesare is then able to print, as an illustration of the houses Vitruvius had in mind, a plan that is as symmetrical as that of Poggioreale or the Palazzo Strozzi, though it is not yet Palladian (fig. 1.16). For clarity's sake we have transcribed only the essentials of the plan—the double grid and the main courtyards. (It is interesting that Cesare calls the plan the "symmetry" of the house. It is as if he were thinking: "symmetry—same measurements—really means: same measurements on either side of an axis.")

Cesare's version of Vitruvius's Roman house, then, is an upright 5:3 rectangular perimeter split into 20-foot squares. Within this grid, and matching it, is a denser one of 10-foot squares. Hence we could call the vertical split sextuple and the horizontal split decuple. These coordinates locate all the minor rooms—wings, *fauces* (entrances), etc.—around the three central rectangles of peristyle, *tablinum* (room joining atrium and peristyle), and *impluvium* (open court for the collection of rainwater). Note that the central axis, as in Poggioreale and as will be the case with Palladio, is a concentric string of rooms.

1.17 *Proportions of Palladio's Roman house plan. After Vitruvius*, I dieci libri dell'architettura tradotti e commentati da Daniele Barbaro, 1567 *(Milan, 1987).*

DANIELE BARBARO

In 1547 Barbaro began working on his editions of Vitruvius (1556, 1567) with his own commentaries and with illustrations by Palladio.[36] These commentaries carry directly on with the tendencies just discussed.[37]

We noted that Vitruvius had said (6.2.1) that houses should be modular, but that he supplied no example and specified no geometrical rules. To remedy this, Barbaro provides a gloss that Vitruvius would certainly never have agreed with. Following Cesare, he says that Vitruvius really meant that the modular system is the same for public buildings as for private houses. He adds that houses should in fact possess the same decorum and beauty we see in public buildings.[38] Much more specifically than Cesare, therefore, Barbaro imbues house design with the proportional rules that Vitruvius gives for temples (3.1ff.). In Barbaro the ancient house is now subject to all sorts of requirements as to length, width, the play of axes, down to the smallest details of ornament. Room is made for use of temple forms—colonnades and frontispieces particularly. Indeed such things are demanded. Barbaro also makes it clear that all this is no antiquarian exercise. Modern clients were to construct and live in these symmetrized versions of Vitruvius's *domus romana.*[39]

Palladio, Barbaro's illustrator, goes even further. He embellishes the discussion with three views of a private palace. The first is an axial section showing the two stories of the house proper and its main courtyard, which, like a true temple, has six colossal Corinthian columns per side. The second view is the palace's plan. This is divided into square and square-derived compartments of various sizes, which form courtyards and rooms.

The plan can therefore be measured neatly out in *ratae partes* as specified by Vitruvius himself. In addition, the plan conforms to the axial principles elaborated by Cesare. The central axis is one 3-module wide and eight long; the cross axis is composed of two groups of three 2-modules, one module wide; and the four intervening blocks are either 3×4 or 3×6 1-modules (fig. 1.17). Alternatively, in line with the procedure we will be using in the next chapter, one can define the plan as a septuple vertical split with ratios of 4:4:4:5:4:4:4 and a horizontal 11-way split with ratios, running from top to bottom, of 4:4:4:4:5:4:4:4:4:4:4. (In a true Palladian plan this type of description becomes a lot less clumsy.)

Barbaro had also said that houses should have the "symmetries," meaning the modular structure, of temples. In fact Palladio's Roman house really is that of a Vitruvian temple with six columns across the front, including a wider center intercolumniation, and eleven columns along the side. The only anomaly is the wider "column" just over halfway back. Thus does the *domus romana* indeed have the "symmetries" of the hexastyle temple described in Vitruvius 3.3.6. Indeed, the house plan could have been traced from the temple plan that Palladio drew to illustrate Vitruvius 3.2.1.[40] Let us note parenthetically that Palladio's six canonical options for rectangular room-shapes, the $\sqrt{2}$:1, 1:1, 4:3, 3:2, 5:3, and 2:1, are identical to those Vitruvius gives for atria, peristyles, triclinia, and exedrae.

Palladio's third view of the Roman house is half of the front elevation (fig. 1.18).[41] This again buttresses Barbaro's claim that the "symmetries" of the temple apply to the house. The elevation may not at first seem out of the ordinary—a typical Palladian facade with a colossal octastyle Corinthian portico flanked by plain, two-story, six-windowed wings.[42] Yet the design proposes to illustrate Vitruvius's Roman house with a type of facade that, at the very most, is rare in ancient Roman architecture. Most Roman houses, even the most luxurious, had little or no architectural ornament on the exterior walls, however gorgeous the interiors. Simple columned porticoes were fairly common. But the addition of the triangular pediment or *fastigium*, creating what looked like the front of a temple on the facade of a private house, was highly unusual, and indeed could be considered suspect and pretentious. Thus Cicero, in the most famous passage on the subject, denounces the presumptuousness of one of his enemies by saying: "this man would have [in his private house] a couch for statues of gods, a pediment, and a priest."[43] In the same vein Alberti inveighs against *fastigia* on private houses on the grounds that they subtract from the majesty proper to churches.[44] Cicero's and Alberti's sentiments certainly go against Barbaro's idea that houses should have

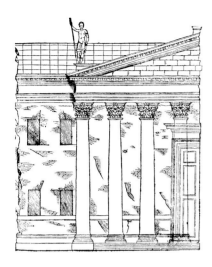

*1.18 Palladio's Roman house facade.
From Barbaro's Vitruvius.*

the same decor as public buildings.[45] But Barbaro's (and Palladio's) powerful misreading of Vitruvius produced a type of house—a Palladian house rather than a *domus romana*, in fact—that has become so commonplace that we fail to see the novelty it possessed when it was introduced.[46]

In short, the Renaissance development of the notion of symmetry—the thing itself if not its name—played a role in the elaboration of Renaissance domestic architecture. To review: beginning with Filarete, mirror symmetry across a vertical axis was considered desirable in a house. Francesco di Giorgio claimed that ancient houses had been similarly symmetrical. Cesare confirmed this and pretended to find a warrant for it in Vitruvius. Daniele Barbaro repeated his predecessors' claims and added that a house should have the same beauty, order, and symmetries as a temple. Finally, Palladio himself illustrated the idea with a house whose plan actually seems to have been based on the plan of a Vitruvian temple, and which also had a temple front and colossal courtyard colonnade. By the end of this whole process, which occurred over a period of less than a century, the "Roman house" had been reinterpreted into something close to the Palladian villa.

But the way in which Renaissance domestic architecture developed its use of symmetry was in fact to differ considerably from Vitruvius's rules for temples. Modules, grids, and the like played their role; canonical volumes were to be found; but the real laws involved the instinctive use of what we now recognize as reflective, bilateral, rotational, and glide symmetry. Our diagrams apply these modern concepts to the Renaissance forms. The first pure examples are Poggioreale and the Strozzi palace. Poggioreale, especially as revamped by Serlio, was a key element in the elaboration of central-plan symmetry, with later reflections in the work of Leonardo and in Palladio's central-plan villas. As we shall see, it is in large part because it obeyed the laws of symmetry, in turn, that Palladio's villa architecture lends itself so well to our type of analysis.

PLANMAKER

2

The corpus of plans we will be studying consists of those in Book II of Palladio's *Quattro Libri* and some of his villa project drawings. Our first goal is simple: to generate plans that are horizontally symmetrical and modular, meaning that they are comprised of rectangles only.[1] To begin, we must translate the rules about symmetry and modularity outlined in chapter 1—rules that, as we saw, can be written in different ways to achieve the same result—into language the computer can use. Planmaker, our computer program for generating plans, will construct its plans by splitting and resplitting the rectangle formed by the building's perimeter into smaller rectangles. We define these splits as lines or sets of lines that divide a rectangular space into any number of smaller rectangular areas.

The direction of a split may be horizontal, vertical, or a combination of both. Any combination split could be reconstituted using a sequence of horizontal and vertical splits. However, we define the combination split as a unique, third variety because it always creates a grid; a sequence of horizontal and vertical splits does not always create a grid. (As we shall see, a grid is often the foundation of a Palladian plan.) Figures 2.1a, b, and c demonstrate the three split directions; figure 2.1d illustrates what will not be defined as splits. As we see in figures 2.1a and b, a split does not necessarily create rooms of equal size. Figure 2.1a also defines how we will use the terms "width" and "length."

Three characteristics define a split: direction—horizontal, vertical, or both—number, and ratio. Number is the number of new rooms created by the split. Figure 2.1a illustrates a triple horizontal split that creates three rooms. Figure 2.1b is a quintuple vertical split, and figure 2.1c a double horizontal split combined with a triple vertical one. The split ratio defines the relative proportions of the new rooms. Using the same split direction and number (referred to in combination as the split type) but varying the ratio, one can divide a room many different ways. Figure 2.2 shows four of the many possible split ratios for a triple vertical split.

a   (width) / (length)   horizontal

b   (width) / (length)   vertical

c   horizontal and vertical

d   not splits

2.1   *Split directions.*

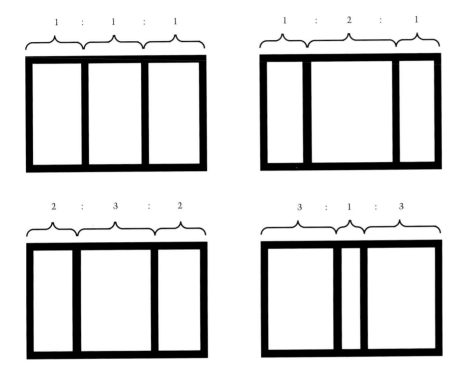

2.2   Some possible split ratios for a triple vertical split.

If we continue the splitting process, it creates what we will call split trees, namely sequential splits done in stages like the generations in a family tree. Split trees are analytic as well as generative devices. We can use them to describe any of Palladio's existing rectangular plans. (As we shall see in chapter 4, we could also split so as to create nonrectangular rooms, but for now we must limit ourselves to the standard rectangular room.)

In figure 2.3 we illustrate the split tree of the plan of the Villa Valmarana at Lisiera (*Quattro Libri*, 2.59). The actual plan is shown in figure 2.3a; the remaining figures illustrate progressive stages of the split tree. The sequence begins with one large horizontal 4:3 area without interior walls (fig. 2.3b).

a

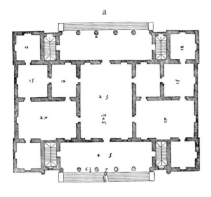

b

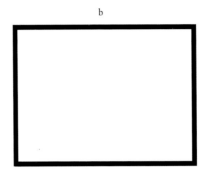

c

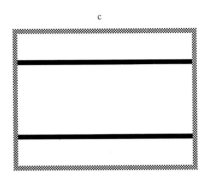

d

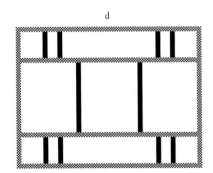

e

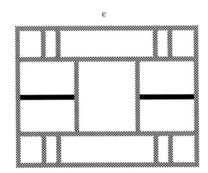

f

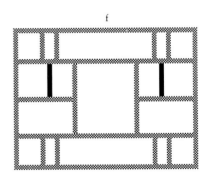

2.3   Left, *split tree for the Villa Valmarana, Lisiera da Balzano Vicentino, from the* Quattro Libri; *right, the corresponding split description.*

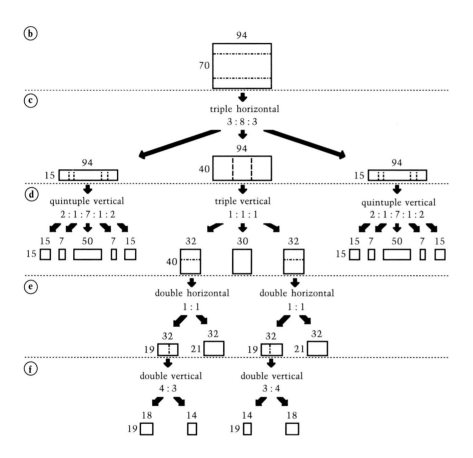

1. In the first stage we map onto 2.3b all continuous interior walls from the original design. (For the present we will ignore doors and windows; they come later.) The Villa Valmarana at Lisiera has two such walls running horizontally its entire width. We isolate them in figure 2.3c. The top and bottom rooms are each as wide (measuring across) as the middle room, but only $\frac{3}{8}$ as long (measuring downward). So our new walls define a triple horizontal split with a ratio of 3:8:3.

2. We now consider independently each new room created by the first split. (We show old splits in gray lines, new ones in black.) There is no obligation to split each of these rooms in the same way, but the same criterion as in the first stage determines what new splits we will identify. For each new room we will include any continuous wall from Palladio's plan that creates smaller rooms within the three spaces in figure 2.3c. Figure 2.3d is the result. It was produced by applying a quintuple vertical split in the top and bottom rooms (in which we simplified the original 15:7:50:7:15 to its close but simpler relative 2:1:7:1:2) and a triple vertical split (with ratio 1:1:1, simplified from 32:30:32) in the middle room.[2]

3. Now another split occurs, a simple double horizontal one, with a ratio of 1:1 (fig. 2.3e). In keeping with the rule for bilateral symmetry, it is identically applied to the two rooms flanking the central space.

4. In the last stage (fig. 2.3f), we split the upper section of each of these flanking rooms vertically, and symmetrically, using the ratio of 4:3; the larger room thus created is on the outside in each case. The original plan of the villa is now completely duplicated.

Let us return for a moment to figure 2.3e. This stage marks the first moment in our process in which certain rooms created by the previous stage were *not* split. These rooms, then, have no further branches in the split tree. Further, as suggested earlier, a single split may be both horizontal and vertical at the same time. In figure 2.4 we see the plan of the Villa Angarano (*Quattro Libri*, 2.46). It has a combination horizontal/vertical split in the first stage (fig. 2.4c) that creates its defining grid (both horizontal and vertical split lines run the full length of the

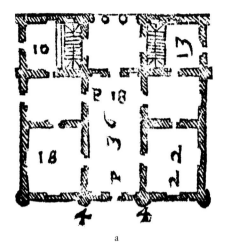

a

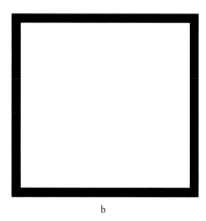

b

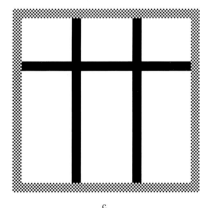

c

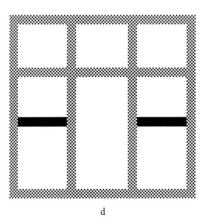

d

2.4 *Split description of the Villa
Angarano, Angarano, from the* Quattro
Libri.

building). By contrast, we used no combination splits in duplicating the Villa Valmarana, and it does not have the same rigid gridlike structure as the Villa Angarano. The rest of figure 2.4 maps out the same process we went through in figure 2.3b–f.

Although we do not know if Palladio actually designed plans using splits, he did use a method of subdivision and resubdivision—splitting—in other arenas. One example is his instructions for generating entablatures; figure 2.5 shows his directions for the Ionic entablature.[3] Our splitting of plans is analogous to Palladio's technique here of beginning with a starting area, subdividing it using a ratio, and then treating each resulting part as an entity that can in turn be subdivided or else left whole. The principal difference is that entablature sections, as here, have only one divisible dimension, height, while plans have both length and width.

Palladio uses this system for laying out a whole range of friezes and entablatures in the *Quattro Libri*. Consequently, he avoids the complex fractions that Vitruvius uses—or rather, he translates those fractions into simple geometrical terms. It is far more comprehensible to use this split system than to say, for example, that the second fascia is $\frac{4}{45}$ of the total height of the entablature, that the modillions are $\frac{10}{93}$ of the total height, and so forth. And for our purposes, it is important to note that just such a sequence, if alternated between horizontal and vertical splits, could be applied to a house plan.

Theoretically, then, we can duplicate Palladio's plans by using the split system. But so far this is simply a way of giving Planmaker a language in which to *describe* Palladian plans. Let us now see if we can engage it in the more complex task of *creating* them. Planmaker will first choose, at random, the length and width of the starting perimeter. It will then pick an arbitrary split type and split ratio, draw out the resulting rooms, and, for each further room, pick another arbitrary split type and ratio, and draw out those resulting rooms. It will continue until the plan is complete.

The architrave, frieze, and cornice [collectively, the entablature] are, as I have said, a fifth part of the height of the column,

the whole to be divided into twelve parts, of which the architrave is four parts, the frieze three, and the cornice five.

The architrave is to be divided into five parts; of one its cymation is made,

and the remaining four divided into twelve parts, [five] of which are given to the first fascia and its astragal, four to the second and its astragal, and [three] to the third.

The cornice is to be divided into seven parts and three fourths; two must be given to the cavetto and ovolo, two to the modillions, and three and three fourths to the corona and gola or cima.

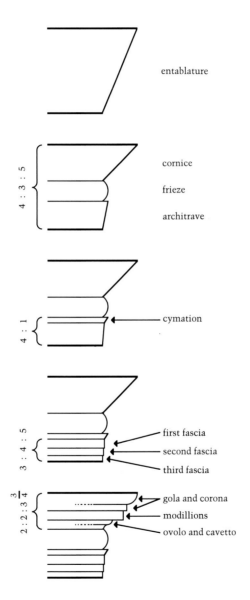

entablature

4 : 3 : 5

cornice

frieze

architrave

4 : 1

cymation

3 : 4 : 5

first fascia

second fascia

third fascia

2 : 2 : 3 : 3¾

gola and corona

modillions

ovolo and cavetto

2.5 *Palladio's instructions for generating an Ionic entablature.* Left, *his text from the* Quattro Libri; right, *the split ratios presented graphically.*

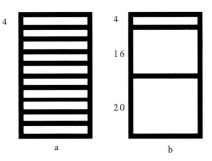

2.6 *Nonsensical split ratios.*

But what split types and ratios should Planmaker choose? There must be some method to our madness. Since Planmaker will operate truly at random, left to its own devices it might happily divide a 20×40 room using a decuple horizontal split, thus creating ten exceedingly narrow rooms each 20 feet long and 4 feet wide (fig. 2.6a)! We must get rid of any tendency to do such things. Planmaker could also make the mistake, after selecting a reasonable split type like triple horizontal, of then choosing a ratio of 1:4:5 (fig. 2.6b)—and again create a worthless room 4 feet long.

To prevent these mistakes we supply Planmaker with fixed lists of possible split types from which to choose (triple horizontal, double vertical, etc.) and possible ratios for each (double splits of 1:1, 1:2, 2:3, etc.; triple splits of 1:1:1, 1:2:1, 2:3:2, etc.). What types and ratios should our lists contain? The answer, of course, lies in the *Quattro Libri.* We compile a split tree description of every relevant plan in Book II. From these trees we then tabulate all possible split types, all possible split ratios, and their statistical frequencies. For example, all basically six-part plans, like figure 2.4, produce trees with a double horizontal/triple vertical split type. Tables 2.1 and 2.2 list our results. These tables, in turn, will serve as a stepping-stone to other rules, rules that govern all of Palladio's plans.

In determining split ratios, however, we encounter the well-known fact that it is hard to get precise measurements and proportions from the illustrations in the *Quattro Libri.* Indeed the rooms in Palladio's plans are rarely split precisely into the ideal ratios shown in table 2.2. It was necessary for us to round off many of the values. For example, if we split a room 44 Vicentine feet wide, as Palladio did in the *Quattro Libri,* into three rooms with widths of 10, 22, and 10 feet, we recorded that ratio as 1:2:1 instead of 5:11:5. Even simple ratios such as 8:3:3 were further rounded, in this case to 3:1:1. In many instances these odd ratios result from having to account for such things as wall thickness or the vagaries of the engraver. In any case, there is no harm in rounding off Palladio's values. As one can see in figure 2.7, at the scale of Palladio's villa plans the eye cannot register the difference between, say, 25:10:8, 8:3:3, and 3:1:1.

TABLE 2.1	
FREQUENCIES OF SPLIT TYPES IN THE *QUATTRO LIBRI*	
SPLIT TYPE	FREQUENCY (%)
Double horizontal	20
Triple horizontal	18
Quadruple horizontal	3
Quintuple horizontal	2
Double vertical	5
Triple vertical	27
Quintuple vertical	7
Double horizontal and triple vertical	8
Double horizontal and quintuple vertical	2
Triple horizontal and triple vertical	5
Quadruple horizontal and triple vertical	3

TABLE 2.2

FREQUENCY OF SPLIT RATIOS IN THE *QUATTRO LIBRI*

DOUBLE RATIOS	%	TRIPLE RATIOS	%	QUADRUPLE RATIOS	%	QUINTUPLE RATIOS	%
1:1	29	1:1:1	25	1:2:2:1	50	1:1:2:1:1	34
4:3	14	1:2:1	25	1:1:1:1	10	2:2:1:2:2	34
3:2	14	2:3:2	13	2:1:1:1	10	2:1:1:1:2	8
2:1	29	3:2:3	13	3:1:1:1	10	2:1:2:1:2	8
3:1	14	1:4:1	6	4:1:1:1	10	2:1:3:1:2	8
		4:1:4	6	5:1:1:1	10	2:1:4:1:2	8
		1:5:1	6				
		5:1:5	6				

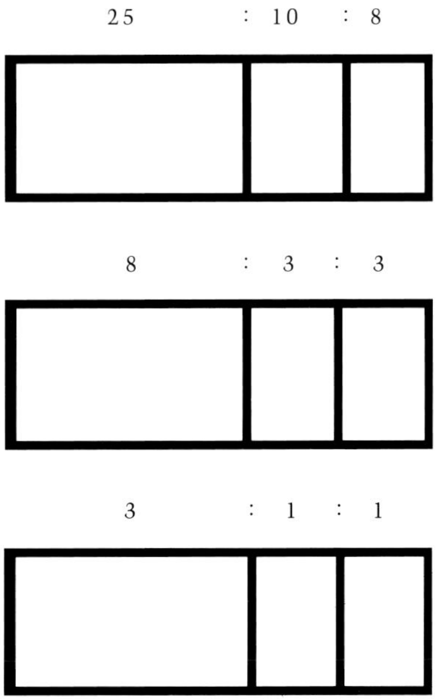

2 5   :   1 0   :   8

8   :   3   :   3

3   :   1   :   1

2.7 *Numerically different but visually identical split ratios.*

But we have not yet addressed one further basic question: When should Planmaker stop splitting? How does it decide between continuing to split and leaving a room whole? To rephrase these questions in more familiar terms, what is the "proper" size of a room? Palladio's answer is vague. Except in one specific instance that we will note shortly, his only instructions regarding room size are that a building should contain "large, middle-sized, and small rooms."[4] Although his specific rules are hazy, his underlying principle, easily observed from the plans themselves, is clear: Villas must contain rooms of logically varying size.[5]

Vitruvius also implies, without giving any very specific directions (except for atria), that in a house the rooms should be of clearly different sizes. As with Alberti and Palladio, Vitruvius's differences are largely based on the rooms' functions. Here we might note one sort of room that puzzles the modern eye: the interior room with no windows. It is found in Palladio's own plans, like figure 2.3a, and will be found in ours as well. Such rooms were used in sixteenth-century villas for storage, toilets, and the like, and also as waiting rooms for servants attending their masters who were using the larger, well-lighted rooms.

And so we will have rooms of properly different sizes. We can base Planmaker's decision to split or not on the area of the room in question. But our guidelines cannot be absolute. None of the quoted authorities specifies how many rooms there should be of each size. For example, if we were to tell Planmaker to split all rooms with areas larger than 800 square feet, then we would eliminate all such large main rooms from its plans and severely restrict variation. We would also be going against Palladio's own example. The problem is solved if Planmaker makes its decisions to split randomly, based on a percentage. It could, for example, split rooms measuring 700 to 1000 square feet 40 percent of the time. Translating this idea into a computer-usable concept, we would have Planmaker, confronted with the decision to split or not to split, pick a random number between 1 and 100 and then split the room in question only if the number were between 1 and 40.

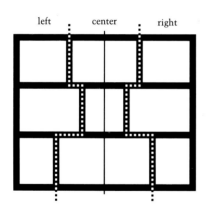

left   center   right

2.8 *Rooms that are to the left of, on, and to the right of the vertical axis of symmetry.*

40

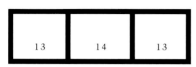

13   14   13

2.9   A sample split.

TABLE 2.3	
SPLIT FREQUENCIES IN THE *QUATTRO LIBRI* BY ROOM SIZE	
ROOM SIZE (SQUARE FEET)	PERCENT SPLIT
<300	3
300–500	20
500–700	22
700–1000	40
>1000	66

We will adjust this percentage, of course, to accord with what we glean from Book II as to the frequency with which Palladio splits rooms with areas between 700 and 1000 square feet. We use the same principle for rooms of all other sizes: for example, how often does Palladio split rooms with areas of less than 300 feet? To collect this information we recycle the split trees that we have already compiled from the Book II plans. For each new room in any stage we now record the room's area and whether or not it was split in the following stage. After dividing the rooms into ranges by area, we calculate the percentage that were split within each range. Table 2.3 lists the results. As one might expect, the smaller the room the less frequently it was split.

But how do we enforce the second principle we mentioned at the outset? Aside from limiting ourselves solely to rectangular rooms, we also opted, in accordance with Palladio's plans, for bilateral reflective symmetry. To achieve it, let us now classify all rooms into one of the three groups shown in figure 2.8: rooms to the left of the vertical axis, rooms lying on that axis, and those to its right. Planmaker will split rooms along the center string as usual. However, it will insist that splits in the left-hand and right-hand room groups be mirror images of each other.

A preliminary example is shown in figure 2.9. Suppose Planmaker is examining a room 40 × 17, or 680 square feet. After selecting the number 19 at random, it splits the room because table 2.3 instructs it to split rooms between 500 and 700 square feet 22 percent of the time. It then chooses a split type, also at random, say triple vertical. Next it selects a ratio for the split type, say 1:1:1. It is impossible to divide the room integrally, so Planmaker divides the 40-foot width into three new rooms respectively 13, 14, and 13 feet wide. To preserve symmetry it adds the extra foot to the center room.

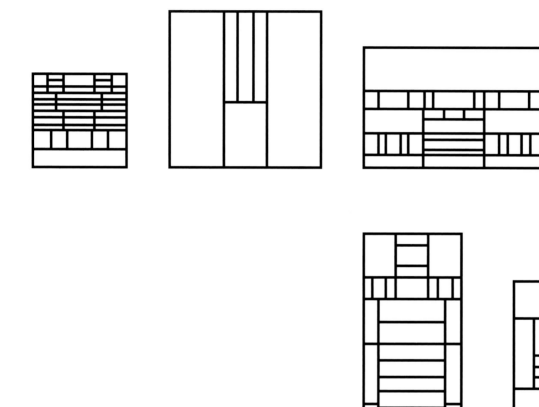

Now that we have instructed Planmaker as fully as possible, for the present anyway, we can begin generating our first set of "Palladian" plans. Planmaker has clear guidelines for all decisions and will operate without our aid. But, as we have warned, we foresee as yet unidentifiable mistakes and hope to learn from them. Sure enough, as soon as Planmaker is let loose using our incipient "Palladian" rules, it comes up with plenty of mistakes from which to learn.

Figure 2.10 illustrates six plans that look more like wall treatments by the art nouveau artist C. R. Mackintosh than like anything by Palladio. (Perhaps that is appropriate, given the type of computer we work with.) And yet the plans do unquestionably conform to our two most fundamental Palladian principles, rectangular rooms and bilateral reflective symmetry.

But the mistakes leap off the page. Our first complaints concern room shapes. These plans contain a plethora of overly stretched, sliver-shaped rooms. Palladio's text offers advice regarding such problems, for as we have noted he lists seven ideal room shapes. These start with the square and move by simple added fractions to a maximum of two squares (i.e., the long dimension equal to twice the short dimension).[6] Although Palladio does occasionally employ spaces of more exaggerated dimensions, usually porches or loggias, rooms of more than two squares are in fact rare. In contrast, the plans that Planmaker is now spewing forth (and these are only a tiny sample) contain many of these overlong room shapes. Splits only consider one dimension at a time and ignore the consequences of the other dimension. Our rules must be more specific.

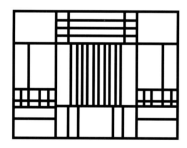

2.10 Planmaker's first group of plans.

We can correct this problem, as usual, by rewriting one of Palladio's own rules for Planmaker. We will demand that it split any room, regardless of size, that is more than two squares in proportion. Yet we know already that the new rule will not work in isolation. For one thing, Palladio does sometimes call for three-square (or three-square-plus) rooms, as in the Villa Valmarana (fig. 2.3a). But suppose, furthermore, that the rule causes Planmaker to split the overly long room in figure 2.11a. Planmaker might well decide as in figure 2.11b to split it vertically into two

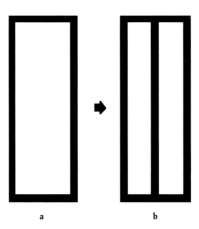

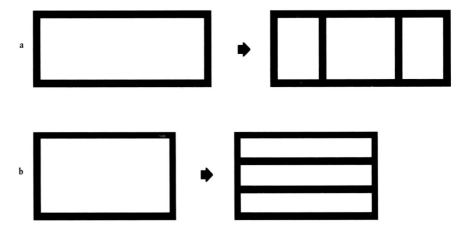

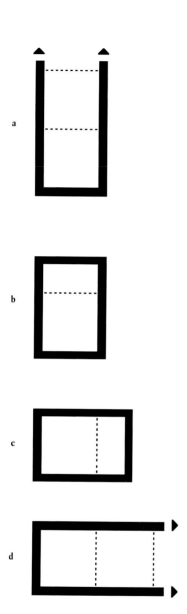

even narrower rooms. In short, Planmaker's method of selecting the split type randomly from a table, without considering the room's proportions, is inadequate. What we need to do is coerce it to "split toward the square," that is, to pick split types such that the resulting rooms are less than two squares. Figure 2.12a illustrates what we consider to be splitting toward the square; figure 2.12b, on the other hand, illustrates what is from now on discouraged.

To put it another way, we are asking Planmaker to pick split types based on the rooms' ratios of length to width. Exactly what should the final proportions of the rooms be? Palladio's six canonical options (we are not considering circles for the moment), we recall, are $\sqrt{2}$:1, 1:1, 4:3, 3:2, 5:3, and 2:1. Since neither we nor Planmaker know which room is to be a loggia as opposed, say, to a courtyard, we will blur these proportions into a continuum. We accordingly divide all rooms into the four categories shown in figure 2.13: length greater than twice the width (a), length less than twice the width but greater than the width (b), width greater than the length but less than twice the length (c), and width greater than twice the length (d).

Hereafter, in contrast to its earlier practice, Planmaker will classify a given room in terms of these categories. Only then will it choose a split type. Each category of proportions, in turn, will require a different set of split types. The split types for categories (a) and (b) should be predominantly horizontal, and those for (c) and (d) predominantly vertical.

To further decide just what split types to choose for each kind of ratio, and what their frequencies should be, we will refine our analysis from table 2.1. We again compile a split tree of every relevant plan in Book II, but we now sort each split type into one of the four new categories of length-width ratio shown in figure 2.13. The final tabulations in table 2.4 show that Palladio's own plans, when interpreted in a computer-friendly way, do in fact have a marked tendency to split toward the square, just as we suggested above. The tendency is not absolute, however: note the frequency of triple vertical split types in category (b), and of double and triple horizontals in category (c). But these anomalies occur, we also

2.13 *The four categories of room length-to-width ratio.*

TABLE 2.4

SPLIT TYPE FREQUENCIES BY CATEGORIES OF
ROOM LENGTH-TO-WIDTH RATIO IN THE *QUATTRO LIBRI*

SPLIT TYPE	FREQUENCY (%)	SPLIT TYPE	FREQUENCY (%)
(A) LENGTH GREATER THAN TWICE WIDTH		(C) WIDTH GREATER THAN LENGTH BUT LESS THAN TWICE LENGTH	
Double horizontal	10	Double horizontal	25
Triple horizontal	20	Triple horizontal	10
Quadruple horizontal	50	Double vertical	10
Quintuple horizontal	20	Triple vertical	15
		Quintuple vertical	5
(B) LENGTH GREATER THAN WIDTH BUT LESS THAN TWICE WIDTH		Double horizontal and triple vertical	25
Double horizontal	27	Triple horizontal and triple vertical	5
Triple horizontal	27	Double horizontal and quintuple vertical	5
Triple vertical	20		
Quadruple horizontal and triple vertical	13	(D) WIDTH GREATER THAN TWICE LENGTH	
Triple horizontal and triple vertical	13	Double vertical	7
		Triple vertical	73
		Quintuple vertical	20

TABLE 2.5	
SPLIT FREQUENCIES IN THE *QUATTRO LIBRI* **FOR ROOMS ON AND OFF THE CENTER AXIS**	
ROOM SIZE (SQUARE FEET)	PERCENT SPLIT
CENTER ROOMS	
<300	0
300–500	24
500–700	21
700–1000	25
>1000	33
OFF-CENTER ROOMS	
<300	4
300–500	17
500–700	22
700–1000	100
>1000	100

note, only in the two middle categories, (b) and (c), where the room shapes are less extreme. Our original rule, then, which forced Planmaker to split all rooms greater than two squares, will now have its intended effect.

But there are more mistakes in the plans in figure 2.10. We now notice their conspicuous lack of a large-scale central focus. Palladio's own plans all center on main spaces—courtyards, rotundas, or oversized rooms—that he refers to as *sale*. They always lie on the center axis. We should once again employ our ability to nudge Planmaker, this time toward larger rooms on the center axis. We nudge rather than force because, following Palladio, not every room lying on the axis is oversized, only most of them. Such central spaces will result if Planmaker splits the rooms along the center axis less frequently than it does other rooms. Again, the answer to the question "how much less often?" lies in a refinement of a previous rule.

Table 2.3 lists the percentages of rooms split, sorted by size. We now break this information down into two categories, one for rooms on the center axis, the other for rooms off it. As previously, we then divide the rooms into ranges by area and calculate the percentage that are split within each range.

Table 2.5 shows the result. Note that the groups of smaller rooms (those less than 700 square feet) are split with roughly the same frequency for center and off-center rooms. Once a center room is split to a small size it no longer serves as a central focus, and so is not treated differently from an off-center room of equivalent size. Conversely, since a larger center room can be a focus, we split it less often than we would its large counterpart that does not not lie on the central axis. Using this table, Planmaker will decide how often to split a room, a decision now based on the room's position relative to the center axis as well as on its size.

Having adjusted the rules so as to insist on rooms less than two squares and to favor, but not insist on, large central spaces, we can now generate our second set of plans. Six samples are shown in figure 2.14. Each has a central focus and there are no sliver-shaped rooms, so we have succeeded in correcting two of Planmaker's

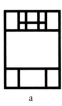
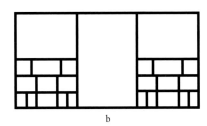

a

b

c

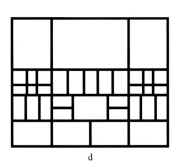
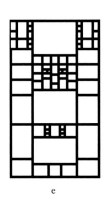
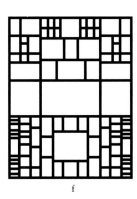

d

e

f

2.14 *Planmaker's second group of plans.*

more wayward tendencies. But now, just as we foretold, the solution of old problems makes new ones obvious.

To begin with, the central rooms in figures 2.14a and b still do not look really Palladian. A quick survey of the Book II villa plans confirms our intuition: none of Palladio's plans contains a rectangular room running the plan's entire length, and only one has a room that stretches the plan's entire width.[7] Most often, rooms that would stretch across the entire length or width of a plan would have to be oblongs greater than two squares, and our previously minted rule therefore tells Planmaker to split them. Occasionally, however, as in figures 2.14a and b, such rooms are not greater than two squares; left to its random devices, Planmaker may legitimately choose not to split them. Therefore, to insure the eradication of these plan-spanning rooms, we will institute a new rule that forces Planmaker to split *any* room that is as long or wide as the entire plan.

Another taboo is broken in figures 2.14c and d. In each plan there is one interior wall that lies directly on the center axis. In fact, both of these walls touch the front facade edge of the plan. As a result, neither of the houses could have a central front door, which in turn would destroy the bilateral symmetry of their main facades. This Palladio would never do. Looking at the plans in Book II once again, we discover no walls lying on center axes, whether touching the facade edge or not. (We do occasionally spot center-axis walls that do not touch the facade edge in, for example, Francesco di Giorgio's symmetrical plans.) Apparently Palladio wanted to preserve the powerful effect of entering a villa and having a sight line straight through the entire building. These offensive, sight line–destroying walls result when Planmaker splits a center room into exact halves using a double vertical split. As a cure, we will prohibit Planmaker from choosing this split type when dividing center rooms.

Lastly, figures 2.14e and f adhere to every rule devised so far, and yet they are still un-Palladian: they have far too many tiny rooms. Planmaker has gone too far in its subdividing. In fact, no room in the Book II plans is less than 40 square feet; some of the rooms in figures 2.14e and f are as small as 15 square feet. The percentages in table 2.5 do strongly discourage Planmaker from splitting small rooms into tiny ones, but recall our other rule, which forces it to split rooms greater than two squares. This rule overrides Planmaker's usual process of choosing whether or not to split, a decision made on the basis of room size. Thus we are inadvertently forcing Planmaker to split small slivers into tiny squares.

We will legislate against these unwanted tiny rooms as follows. Assume Planmaker has decided to split a room and has chosen a split type and ratio. It will then look ahead and calculate the dimensions of the resulting rooms. If any dimension is less than 7 feet it will choose a new split type and ratio. If, after several attempts, it still has not selected a satisfactory type/ratio combination, it will then abandon its attempt to split the room and let it be.

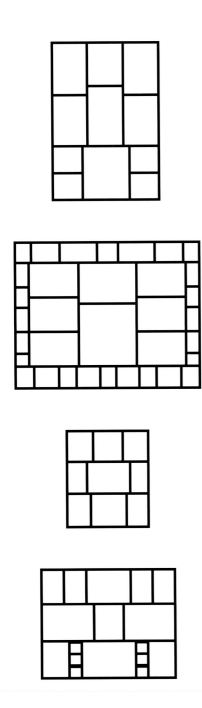

But now we return to an earlier problem. Suppose the old rule forces Planmaker to try to split a room greater than two squares. Then, in accordance with the new rule, after several unsuccessful attempts to choose a proper split type and ratio, it decides not to split the room. Does the old rule override the new, or vice versa? In other words, which is worse, a misshapen room or an undersized one? The answer is that while we find no tiny rooms in Palladio's plans, we do, on rare occasions as noted, find rooms that are "too long." When forced to choose between the two evils, then, Planmaker will opt for the sliverlike but larger room.

Having unmasked three more Palladian taboos, and having instructed Planmaker not to violate them, we now commission it to produce a third set of plans. Four samples are illustrated in figure 2.15. Although they do conform to all the rules identified so far, most observers would probably again classify these plans as un-Palladian. Their Palladian source is clear, but they lack a certain rigor that we will now have to define.

Let us compare a specific Book II plan with the entire step-by-step process by which we can now generate one of our "school of Palladio" arrangements. On the left in figure 2.16a is the plan of the Villa Zeno (*Quattro Libri*, 2.49). In the right-hand column is an approximation of that plan that was randomly generated by Planmaker using all the laws we have formulated so far, but still lacks that undefined Palladian rigor. Although not precisely the same as those in the Villa Zeno, the rooms in the computer-generated plan are all of acceptable dimension, size, and position. So the rigor we are searching for probably does not concern the characteristics of individual rooms. Rather, it seems to concern how rooms relate to each other.

Let us suppose for a moment that the Villa Zeno *had* been computer-generated. By simultaneously retracing the splits that Planmaker would have used to create that plan (the left-hand plan of each pair) and the splits it actually did use to generate the plan at right in each pair, we can detect the point at which the two plans diverge. Figure 2.16b illustrates the starting areas. The first splits are both double horizontal (figure 2.16c). The proportions in the right plan, although

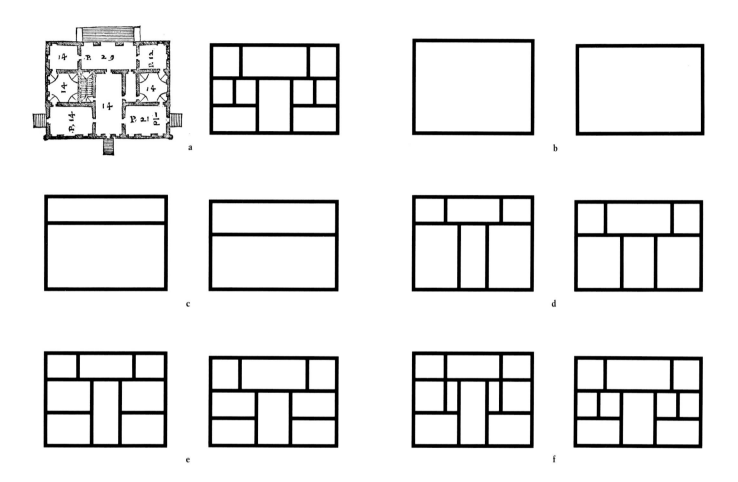

2.16   *Split descriptions of the Villa Zeno,
Donegal di Cessalto (Treviso)* (at left in
each pair), *from the* Quattro Libri; *a
Planmaker plan* (at right in each pair).

different, are acceptable, so we proceed to figure 2.16d. The room-to-room relationships are still the same, as they also are after the next split in figure 2.16e. So we advance to the fourth and final set of splits (fig. 2.16f).

Now we notice a distinct difference between the two plans. In Palladio's plan, the newly added walls align with existing vertical walls. In Planmaker's plan, on the right, they do not. Palladio's plan is more than a mere symmetrical bundling of smaller rectangles within a larger one. Established walls have a tendency—a *tendency*, not an absolute obligation—to continue when new rooms are added, even if there is an interruption between old and new wall. (Note that the question of alignment affects vertical subdivisions more often than horizontal, because mirror symmetry already assures most crosswise wall alignment.)

As Wittkower and others have pointed out, Palladio's plans conform to underlying grids.[8] But in designing plans room by room, as we have been doing, there has been no consideration of such a grid. Let us call this focus on the design of a single room "microstyle." For example, when Vitruvius describes the Roman house he speaks exclusively in terms of microstyle; he is concerned only with the size and proportion of individual rooms. What we will call "macrostyle," on the other hand, embodies the relationship of room to room and of room to whole. When we think of macrostyle in a villa, the key elements are conformity to an underlying grid, enclosure of the plan in a rectangular envelope, and, of course, symmetry.

Until the fifteenth century, macrostyle in this sense applied only to public buildings. Unlike the temple, basilica, or bath, the Roman house, as we have noted, was nearly always irregularly bounded, ungridded, and asymmetrical. We might say that chapter 1 of this book showed how Renaissance architects attempted to infuse domestic architecture with the macrostyle of public architecture. Indeed Palladio defines what we call macrostyle when he writes on the first page of the *Quattro Libri*: "Beauty will result from the form and correspondence of the whole, with respect to the several parts, of the parts with regard to each other, and these again to the whole; that the structure may appear an entire and complete body, wherein each member agrees with the other."[9] "Parts with regard to each other, and these again to the whole" is the definition of macrostyle. And Palladio applies this definition to *every* "fabrick," not just to public structures. Yet as we saw earlier, microstyle cannot be ignored. After all, it is explicitly Vitruvian, and its concentration on variety of room shapes is what keeps villas from becoming monotonous grids. Macrostyle in domestic planning, which is *not* Vitruvian (but became Vitruvian via the reinterpretations of Cesariano, Barbaro, and Palladio), restricts variety because it encourages uniformity of interior spaces. In injecting macrostyle into domestic architecture, therefore, Renaissance architects created a conflict between variety and uniformity that had previously not existed. Palladio's work elegantly resolves this conflict, though he may be observed struggling. (Anyone who doubts the intensity of the struggle should try teaching a computer to mimic Palladian plans and facades. It is a constant battle between anarchy and monotony.)

The limitations on the architect in this struggle between microstyle and macrostyle, then, first involve setting a plan into a rectangular boundary, which is much harder than creating a free-form bundle of rooms. Bilateral symmetry then cuts the architect's field of choice roughly in half. But macrostyle's constantly implied underlying grid is the most constricting demand of all. One can partially mediate between variety and conformity by using a flexible grid—that is, a grid containing modules of various sizes, as in some of the plans illustrated in chapter 1. Palladio uses this approach in the Villa Emo (figure 4.31) and the Palazzo Antonini (figure 4.32). To resolve the conflict using a flexible grid only, however, is Procrustean. Palladio only does this in the two examples cited. If the flexible grid is the architect's only tool, then his role is reduced to that of deciding on the scale of the grid.

Palladio therefore employs more than just a flexible grid. In their article "The Palladian Grammar," Stiny and Mitchell construct grids of squares ranging from 3×3 to 7×5. The grid in figure 2.17a is a 5×3 example. Having set up this matrix, they then simply remove walls, as in figure 2.17b, or shift walls, as in figure 2.17c, until a given plan from the *Quattro Libri* has been replicated.[10]

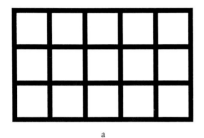 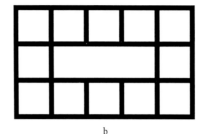 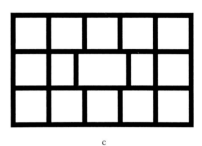

a   b   c

2.17 *Challenging the grid: a 5 × 3 grid (a);*
walls removed (b); walls shifted (c).

This method nicely highlights the struggle between variety and conformity, micro- and macrostyle. Wall removal creates variety in room sizes by catenating two spaces into one, but only mildly violates the grid because it creates merely a temporary break. Wall shifting provides much greater flexibility in proportioning and sizing rooms, but it violates the grid more egregiously. In figure 2.17c the wall shift flouts the grid's very existence. Of the two methods, Palladio uses wall removal more often than wall shifting, but he does shift with some frequency. His most pronounced use of wall shifting is in the now-destroyed Villa Sarego at Miega di Cologna (fig. 2.18; *Quattro Libri*, 2.68), where the horizontal walls in particular are situated without heed to an underlying grid.

Our splitting method, on the other hand, is inherently microstylistic. Since it only considers one room at a time, it often utterly fails to make the "parts," as Palladio says—i.e., the rooms—correspond to each other and to the whole. Until now, therefore, Planmaker has been completely unconcerned with aligning walls to an underlying grid as an end in itself. Only rarely, and by chance, do two walls align in the plans we have generated so far. Our next task, then, defines the architect's conflict: how do we align walls in such a way as to preserve variety of room shapes and not turn our plans into monotonous grids?

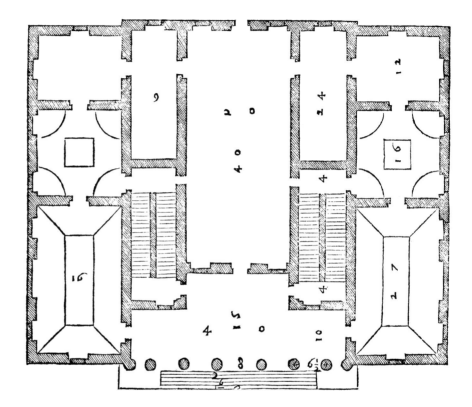

2.18   *An example of wall shifting: the*
Villa Sarego, Miega di Cologna Veneta,
from the Quattro Libri.

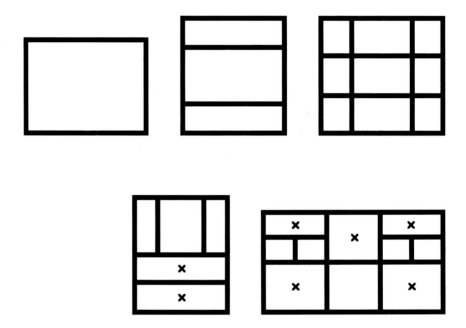

To begin with, many existing rooms do not actually have walls with which new walls may be aligned. In these cases, Planmaker must still be free to choose its split type and ratio at random. Figure 2.19 shows a number of partially completed plans. In any room containing an X, Planmaker would calculate the split type and ratio so as to align the new walls with old walls. In all other rooms it would select the split data at random, and its decision, as before, would be based on the proportions of the room in question.

However, Planmaker should not split rooms simply because it has the opportunity to create aligned walls. Nor should the number of surrounding walls influence Planmaker's decision as to whether or not to split a room. Only *after* making a decision to split will Planmaker check for surrounding walls with which the new walls might or might not align. If there are such walls, Planmaker, in

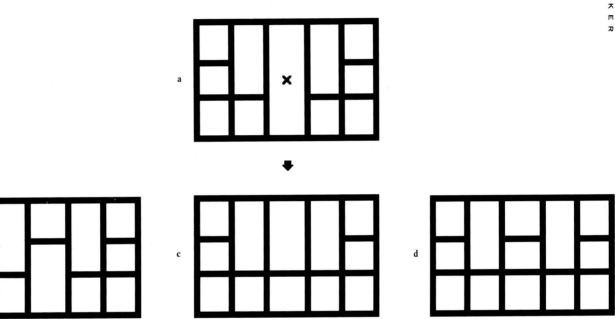

2.20 *Choices for wall alignment.*

most cases overriding its usual random process for choosing a split type and ratio, will align the new walls with some existing wall. To retain the variation we find in Palladio, it will choose at random how many aligning walls it will create—and hence how many new rooms. In figure 2.20a the room marked X is an obvious candidate for splitting. Figures 2.20b–d illustrate Planmaker's three options. Finally, however, Palladio does sporadically "misalign" walls. And so, on random occasions, Planmaker will deliberately do the same. It will ignore surrounding walls and its own tendency toward alignment, choosing a split type and ratio at random.

Having established the practice of wall alignment, we commission a fourth set of plans from Planmaker. Some of these invite comparison with Palladio. Now that we have developed a satisfactory formula, we have the potential to create millions

2.21 *Planmaker plans and their Palladian counterparts: the Villa Cornaro, Piombino Dese (Treviso) (a), from the* Quattro Libri; *a drawing for the Villa Pisani, Montagnana (b), British Architectural Library, RIBA, London, Palladio XVI, 21r; a design for a Tuscan atrium from the* Quattro Libri *(c); a computer-generated plan with no close Palladian analogue (d).*

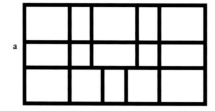

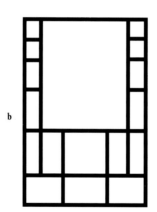

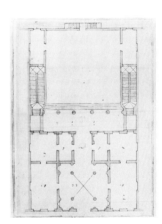

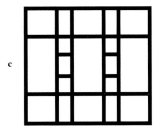

c

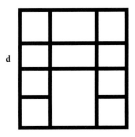

d

of these "Palladian" plans. Since Palladio himself only produced a tiny proportion of all possible Palladian plans, most of the new designs will not have direct analogues in his oeuvre. In the four examples illustrated in figure 2.21, Planmaker's plan is on the left; in three cases (2.21a, b, c), the closest Palladian parallel is on the right.

In figure 2.21a Planmaker has transformed the Villa Cornaro by filling in its L-shaped side wings, eliminating the upper layer of three spaces—a pair of oval stairs flanking a porch—and horizontally subdividing the square tetrastyle hall in the center. A Palladio drawing is on the right in figure 2.21b; Planmaker's scheme on the left continues the line of the stairs partially into the reapportioned body of the villa. The left-hand plan in figure 2.21c abstracts Palladio's interpretation on the right of a Roman house with a "Tuscan atrium" (*Quattro Libri*, 2.18). It further idealizes his already idealized interpretation by making it reflectively symmetric across both the horizontal and vertical axes, and by aligning it more rigorously with the underlying grid. Figure 2.21d has no close analogue, but its inspiration is clear.

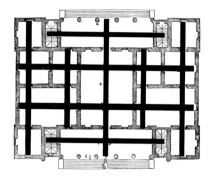

2.22 *Door axes in the Villa Valmarana,*
Lisiera da Balzano Vicentino, from the
Quattro Libri.

We now examine two last elements of Palladio's villa-planning practice: doors and windows. As one might expect, Palladio does not locate them arbitrarily. Their placement is subject to precise lateral symmetry and alignment[11] and derives directly from the placement of walls. Thus doors and windows add another layer of geometric structure to the plans.

Palladio's openings, whether doors or windows, almost invariably lie on major or minor axes. Figure 2.22 illustrates this in the Villa Valmarana at Lisiera (*Quattro Libri*, 2.59). Note that each axis coordinates with a wall: major axes run parallel and adjacent to major walls, while minor axes do the same with shorter walls. The only exceptions, the top and bottom horizontal axes, do not stretch the entire width of the plan because they are blocked by stairs, and Palladio's stairs only have one entrance per floor. However, note that beyond the sets of stairs there are outer windows lying along the same axes. Finally, most of these axes symmetrically bisect the smallest room in their path.

Palladio's other plans show the same hierarchy of major and minor walls, along with associated door axes, that we see in the plan of the Villa Valmarana. We have seen that the language of splits is similarly hierarchical. A split tree, after all, can hardly be otherwise. The succession of walls and axes, then, follows naturally from the split analysis of a given plan. Major walls are those comprising early-stage splits; minor walls appear in later stages. Each new room created by a split should therefore contain a door axis that bisects the room and parallels the new wall.

This being so, Planmaker can simultaneously generate door axes as it splits rooms. Later, after finishing its plan, it can use the door axes to cut openings through the walls. Figure 2.23 illustrates how Planmaker does this. The starting area, shown in figure 2.23a, contains one axis cutting vertically through the top wall, down the center, and through the bottom wall. Superimposition of this axis on the completed plan will create front and back entrances as well as a line of doors running down the center of the villa.

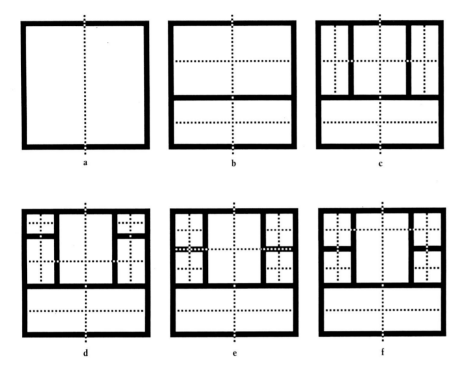

2.23   *Creating door axes.*

Except in one specific case discussed below, we will create a door axis for each new room. Bisecting the new room, the axis parallels the direction of the split that created the room and is exactly as long as the wall that has just been created. All door axes, except the initial vertical one, run to, but not through, the end walls of their corresponding rooms. Figure 2.23b illustrates the first split and the axes created along with it.

Figure 2.23c illustrates a triple vertical split of the top room. We create new door axes for each new room except the center room. (Here is the exception mentioned above; an existing axis already runs through the center room, so a new, shorter axis is redundant.) Note that the top horizontal axis created in the previous split now does puncture two walls. In figure 2.23d we split the top left room using a 1:2

ratio (and reflect this split on the right). We create a door axis along with this upper new room. But, since an existing axis runs through the lower new room, once again we do not create a shorter duplicate. We do, however, shift this existing axis down into the center of the lower room. This is because, as noted, Palladio situates most axes, regardless of their length, so as to bisect the smallest room in their paths.

Returning to figure 2.23c, suppose that we executed the split of the top left and top right rooms with a 1:1 ratio instead of the 1:2 ratio used to create figure 2.23d. Now the new walls land directly on an existing door axis, as shown in figure 2.23e. Subsequent use of this axis would have the unintended result of erasing the entire wall. This conflict is resolved by shifting the axes up to the centers of the new top left and top right rooms, as shown in figure 2.23f. In splitting the top center room, however, Planmaker could again choose a split type and ratio that would place a wall in conflict with the recently moved axis. Given this scenario, it would reject that split type and ratio and select another. Planmaker will shift door axes only once. Otherwise, it could shift them back into conflict with existing walls.

Planmaker deals only in apertures in walls. We are the ones who read the central apertures in the back and front walls, and all apertures inside the house, as doors. We have yet to carve windows. Although most of these will lie on axis with doors, window placement on the main facade (always the bottom edge of the plan) is determined only partially by the plan itself. The facade elevation, as we shall see, is also a determinant. For example, it determines the width of all windows. In the next chapter we will define lines of communication through which facade and plan may amicably negotiate the question of window placement.

We have completed our study of Palladian villa plans. Our search has revealed the following rules:

• Nearly exclusive use of rectangular rooms

• Bilateral symmetry on the central vertical axis

• Doors and windows on axes parallel and adjacent to walls

- Wall alignment where possible

- Larger rooms on the central vertical axis

- No rooms greater than two squares

- No rooms as wide or long as the entire plan

- No room dimension less than 7 Vicentine feet

- No walls along the central vertical axis

How comprehensive is this list? Are there elements we have failed to discover? In chapter 4 we will examine a set of computer-generated plans and facades ranging from the abjectly failed to the startlingly successful. We will also explore the wisdom, value, and limits of computer-based geometric analysis of Palladio's villas.

Adding facades to Palladio's domestic plans is less difficult than creating the plans themselves. Daniele Barbaro's maxim "Every three-dimensional form is born from its plan as a tree is born from its roots" embodies the process we use to recreate Palladio's facades.

Although Planmaker and Facademaker are computer programs, we can imagine them as a pair of architects interacting as they design a Palladian villa. Decisions as to when the exigencies of the facade must override those of the plan, and vice versa, are arrived at by mutual agreement. As much as possible, our own priorities mirror Palladio's. Although he eliminated most conflicts between plan and facade by working the two into a unified whole, traces of compromise remain. Our charge to achieve "all possible Palladian villas" means that for any one plan we will design not one but a multitude of facades. By doing so, interestingly, we encounter conflicts rarely found in Palladio's own designs.

Reflecting their different responsibilities, Planmaker and Facademaker employ opposing methods of design. Planmaker divides and redivides a given rectangle, while Facademaker adds one element to another. The former speaks the language of splits, which as we have seen is a flexible one indeed. In contrast, Facademaker uses a small set of what we call "blocks." A few simple rules guide it in assembling these blocks. Unlike Planmaker, which operates on a blank slate and can produce millions of possibilites, Facademaker is guided and constrained by a preexisting plan and is capable of far fewer variations. As in the last chapter, we have used Book II of the *Quattro Libri* as our primary source. We have, however, also borrowed extensively from Palladio's drawings and built structures.

First of all, then, we must de- and reconstruct the facades in question by viewing them as assemblages, or stacks, of blocks. After identifying all the types of blocks, we will define their possible combinations. Both the types and the combinations are, of course, derived from Palladio. Depending on the particular combination, Facademaker will adjust each block to the plan and then insert it into the facade.[1]

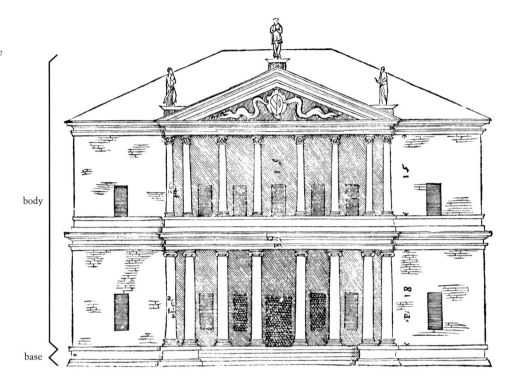

3.1   Base and body on a facade from the Quattro Libri*: Villa Sarego, Miega di Cologna Veneta.*

body

base

We begin by dividing the facade into two sections, base and body. These are illustrated in figure 3.1 for the Villa Sarego at Miega di Cologna (*Quattro Libri*, 2.68). Bases are complex subfacades in their own right, and so we will examine them later. Figure 3.2 illustrates assorted combinations of the four types of body blocks: floor (as in "first floor" or "second floor"), entablature, attic or mezzanine, and roof. A facade need not contain all these block types, and may contain multiple floors or entablatures (fig. 3.2a). The minimal body (fig. 3.2c) consists only of a floor and a roof. In short, our facades simply recombine these four types of blocks.

The essential component of all facades is the floor block. Always located directly above the base, and either one or two stories high, the floor block is the facade's

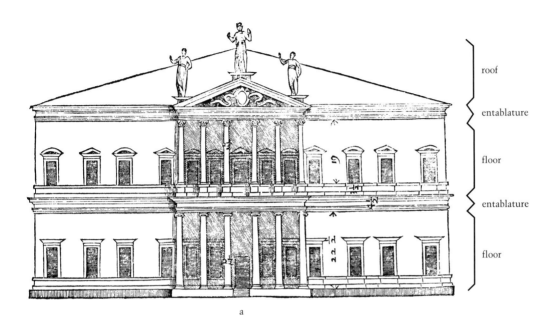

roof

entablature

floor

entablature

floor

a

roof

attic

floor

b

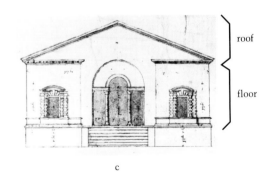

roof

floor

c

3.2   *Different block types: Palazzo Trissino, Vicenza (*a*), from the* Quattro Libri; *the Villa Caldogno, Caldogno (*b*); the Villa Valmarana, Vigardolo di Monticello (*c*), drawing from the British Architectural Library, RIBA, London, Palladio XVII, 2r.*

a

column
block

3.3 *Floor block types: the Villa Emo, Fanzolo (Treviso)* (a); *Palazzo Della Torre, Verona* (b), *from the* Quattro Libri; *the Villa Barbaro, Maser* (c); *the Villa Saraceno, Finale di Agugliaro* (d), *from the* Quattro Libri; *the Villa Zeno, Donegal di Cessalto (Treviso)* (e), *from the* Quattro Libri.

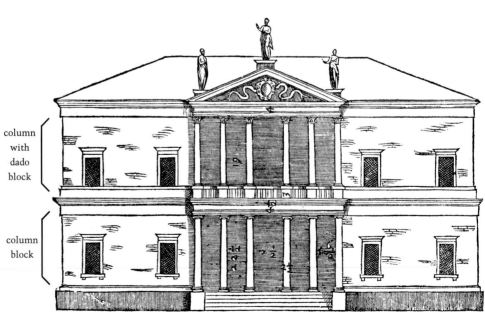

b

column
with
dado
block

column
block

colossal
column
block

c

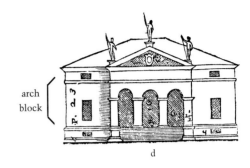

arch
block

d

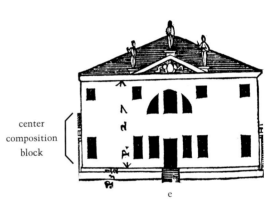

center
composition
block

e

largest, most detailed, and most prominent block. Figure 3.3 illustrates the five different floor blocks found among Palladio's villa facades. We call them: (a) column, (b) column with pedestal or dado, (c) colossal column (more than one story high), (d) arch, and (e) center composition.

Palladio's workhorse, the column block (i.e., either a temple front or a colonnade), forms the first story of his many temple-fronted villas and palazzos. Its close relative (used for the upper story of his temple fronts) is the column with dado block. In it, a dado rests beneath correspondingly shortened columns. The colossal column block is two stories tall, its columns reaching from base to entablature without an intervening cornice or dado. The arch block substitutes arches for columns and is, like the column block, one story high. The center composition block includes all Palladio's villa facades that are neither columnar nor arcuated; it comes in several varieties (fig. 3.4).[2]

a

3.4 *Varieties of center composition: a project drawing (a), from the British Architectural Library, RIBA, London, Palladio XVII, 1r; the Villa Poiana, Poiana Maggiore (b); the Villa Valmarana, Vigardolo di Monticello (c), from Puppi,* Andrea Palladio; *the Villa Pisani at Bagnolo di Lonigo (d), photograph by Philip Trager, reproduced from Trager,* The Villas of Palladio.

b

c

d

3.5 *Entablature blocks: Palazzo*
Garzadore, Vicenza (a), from the Quattro
Libri; *the Villa Badoer, Fratta Polesine*
(Rovigo) (b).

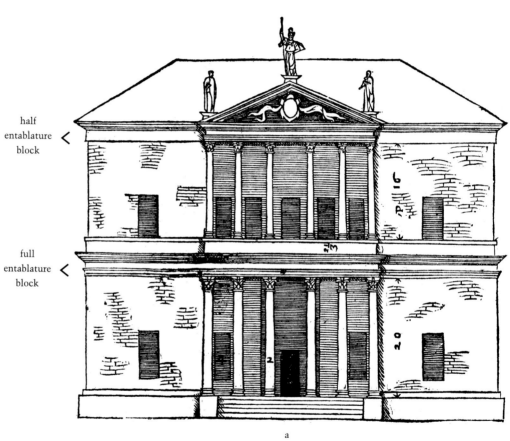

half
entablature
block

full
entablature
block

a

half
entablature
block
containing
windows

>

b

In figure 3.5a we illustrate examples of the two kinds of entablature blocks (*Quattro Libri*, 2.68). The molded stringcourses across the facade distinguish the full entablature (below) from the half entablature (above). These terms are only conveniences, of course; the actual difference is that the full entablature includes an architrave while the half entablature has none. Unlike the full entablature, the half entablature may house windows, as in the Villa Badoer (fig. 3.5b).

Attic blocks are generally one-third the height of floor blocks, and they appear as second or mezzanine stories. The plain attic block on the Villa Forni-Cerato (fig. 3.6a) houses only windows. The Villa Rotonda (fig. 3.6b) has an attic block containing windows and also the pediment of the temple front. Note that the pediment is the full height of the attic block. In addition, some attic blocks in Palladio's facades have no windows in their center section, as in the Villa Saraceno (fig. 3.6d).

*3.6 Attic blocks: the Villa Forni-Cerato,
Montecchio Precalcino (a), from Puppi,* An-
drea Palladio; *the Villa Rotonda, Vicenza
(b); the Villa Valmarana, Lisiera da
Balzano Vicentino (c); the Villa Saraceno,
Finale di Agugliaro (d).*

a

b

c

d

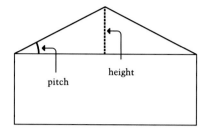

3.7   *Roof pitch and height defined.*

3.8   *Relationship between roof pitch and height.*

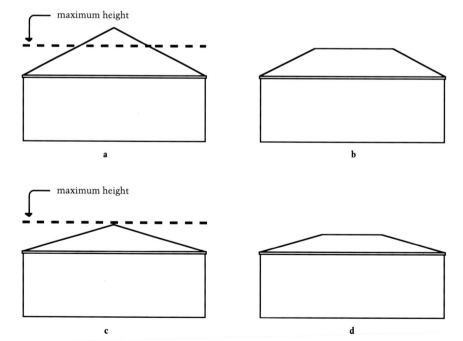

Roof blocks are flexible in size and shape. Two characteristics define a roof, pitch and height, as illustrated in figure 3.7. Most roof pitches in the *Quattro Libri* range from 15° to 35°, so these angles are our minimum and maximum pitches. But Palladio also gives verbal instructions for roof heights. In Book I he writes that the ideal roof height is $\frac{2}{9}$ the width of the facade. However, only about half of the *Quattro Libri* roofs follow this rule. The other half vary, as do our roof heights, between $\frac{1}{9}$ and $\frac{1}{4}$ the width of the facade. Nearly all *Quattro Libri* roofs fall in this range.

Even within these limits, however, the two roof characteristics are not independent variables. The pitch in figure 3.8a is within bounds, but the height exceeds the maximum of $\frac{1}{4}$ of the building's width. A roof this steeply pitched would have to be hipped, as in figure 3.8b. A more moderately pitched roof could be either pyramidal (fig. 3.8c) or hipped (fig. 3.8d), depending on one's choice of roof height. By varying pitch and height within these Palladio-derived limits, we can create a multitude of canonical roofs for any facade.

In figure 3.9 we illustrate the two kinds of roof block, with and without pediment, respectively on the villas Mocenigo at Marocco and Godi. The width of the pediment in figure 3.9b, as we shall see, is fixed by the plan. For the most part Palladio makes the pitch of the pediment equal that of the roof. But while roof pitches vary from 15° to 35°, pediment pitches vary only between 25° and 30°. So if the roof is steeper than 30° or flatter than 25°, we pitch the pediment at a different angle from the roof to keep it within range. These adjustments are shown in figure 3.10.

Finally, the main body of a villa facade must rest on a base. Palladio's base designs are numerous and are related to the villa's site. For example the Villa Foscari (La Malcontenta), sited on a plain adjacent to the river Brenta, sits on an extremely high 11-foot platform to prevent the *piano nobile* from flooding. Other bases are relatively low, and of course urban palazzi typically have no bases at all. To allow for this diversity we need a flexible block—a "superblock," so to speak. If our block description is to be reasonably terse, however, we have to give up the idea

roof
block
without
pediment

a

3.9   *Roof blocks: the Villa Godi, Lonedo (a), photo Scala/Art Resource; the Villa Mocenigo, Marocco (b), from the* Quattro Libri.

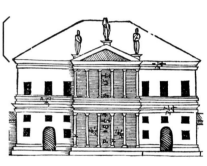

roof
block
with
pediment

b

3.10   *Roof and pediment pitches.*

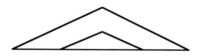

roof pitch = 27°

pediment pitch = 27°

roof pitch > 30°

pediment pitch = 30°

roof pitch < 25°

pediment pitch = 25°

TABLE 3.1			
ALLOWABLE NUMBER			
OF STEPS PER LEVEL			
NUMBER OF LEVELS	NUMBER OF STEPS IN LEVEL		
	1	2	3	4
1	2–4			
2	1–2	2–8		
3	1	3–6	1–3	
4	1	3–6	1–2	2–3

of replicating all of Palladio's bases. We will consider only what we call straight-run bases, and eliminate those bases with steps that are both perpendicular and parallel to the facade. Our aim, which has been to create the rules for all possible Palladian villas, must here be slightly deflected.

Our standard unit of base construction is a set of steps, or a level, defined by a stringcourse. As illustrated in figure 3.11 in four facades from the *Quattro Libri*, bases may consist of from one to four levels. Table 3.1 defines the number of steps each level may contain. The allowable numbers of steps vary with the number of levels in the base as a whole. Although they do not encompass all of Palladio's bases, our step parameters do closely reflect most of his step groupings. In addition, the second base level, if tall enough, may contain windows, as in figure 3.11c.

Like levels, individual steps come in assorted sizes and styles. Accordingly, we define four step characteristics: height, configuration, termination, and width. As illustrated in figure 3.12, each of these characteristics may assume one of two guises: single or double height, straight or splayed configuration, ended or not-ended termination, and broad or narrow width. (We call "step ends" what are more technically dwarf walls—low blocks protruding at right angles from the facade that provide parapets for the stairs.) Note that the combination of guises affects every step, regardless of the number of levels or number of steps per level.

The different combinations of these guises define different base styles. For example, the style in figure 3.11c is single/straight/ended/broad. As shown in figure 3.13, the combination of broad, splayed, and ended is nonsensical because the steps would spread past their terminating ends. For this reason we disallow the combinations single/splayed/ended/broad and double/splayed/ended/broad. Four characteristics, each able to assume one of two guises, minus two combinations, result in fourteen different base styles. We illustrate all of them in figure 3.14 using three-level bases.

3.11   *Base levels 1–4 in* Quattro Libri
designs: the Villa Valmarana, Lisiera da
*Balzano Vicentino (*a*); the Villa Pisani,*
*Montagnana (*b*); the Villa Cornaro,*
*Piombino Dese (Treviso) (*c*); the Palazzo*
*Chiericati, Vicenza (*d*).*

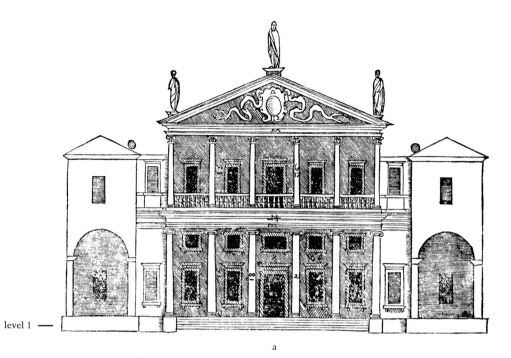

level 1 ——

a

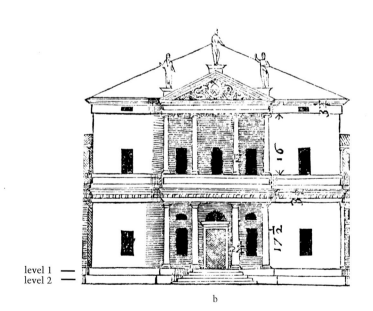

level 1 ——
level 2 ——

b

c

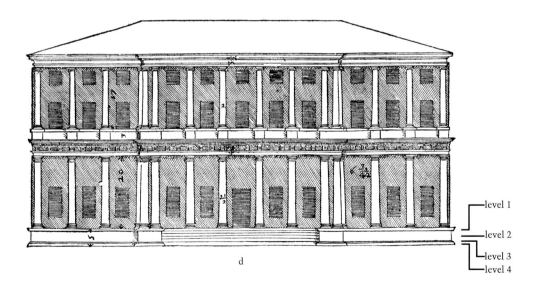

d

3.12 Base characteristics.

Step height

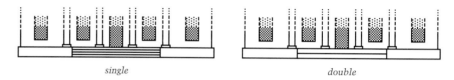

single   *double*

Step configuration

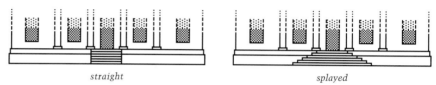

straight   *splayed*

Step termination

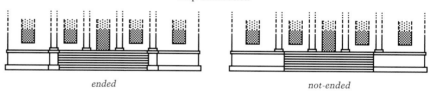

ended   *not-ended*

Step width

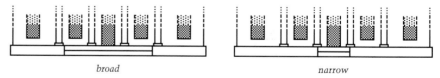

broad   *narrow*

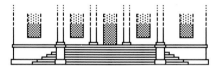

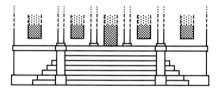

We now possess a full set of blocks. As they stack together in an infinite number of ways, we need to segregate the combinations, or styles, that rate as Palladian. If our definition of "Palladian" is too inclusive then the term loses its meaning; if too exclusive, it defines only part of what Palladio thought possible. So we have to sort through all the possible combinations and accept or refuse them based on Palladio's built, published, and drawn works.

To begin with, common sense excludes many combinations (such as two entablatures stacked one atop the other). Convention dictates many other restrictions. For example, all facades contain one roof and one base block. All arcuated or columnar facades contain exactly one pediment, located in either a roof or an attic block. Arch and column blocks always support an entablature, but center composition blocks never do. Correspondingly, entablatures rest only on arch or column blocks. And we use attic blocks for second stories only, never for ground floors.

Some classically acceptable combinations are not found in Palladio's oeuvre, however, and this poses a dilemma. For one, Palladio pairs a symmetrical plan with a three-story facade only once in the *Quattro Libri* (and the design is for a palazzo, not a villa). Yet we can build myriad three-story villas from our blocks, and in doing so fabricate a sizable class of facades not grounded in Palladio's own work. We do not wish to form the majority of our facades from extrapolations, and so we limit all combinations to two stories or less. Also, the half-entablature block, which may contain windows, must lie underneath the roof and not between stories. Of all Palladio's many one-and-a-half- and two-story facades, not one sandwiches a half entablature between floors. As illustrated in figure 3.15, the entablature windows would disjoin the first and second floors and clutter the facade. We can see why Palladio avoided this particular device.

Lastly, although some of Palladio's arcuated temple fronts are one and a half stories, none are two full stories. From our blocks, however, we can build three such facades, as illustrated in figure 3.16. The absence of facades like that in figure 3.16a from Palladio's entire domestic oeuvre is conspicuous because his basilica

3.14 *The fourteen base styles.*

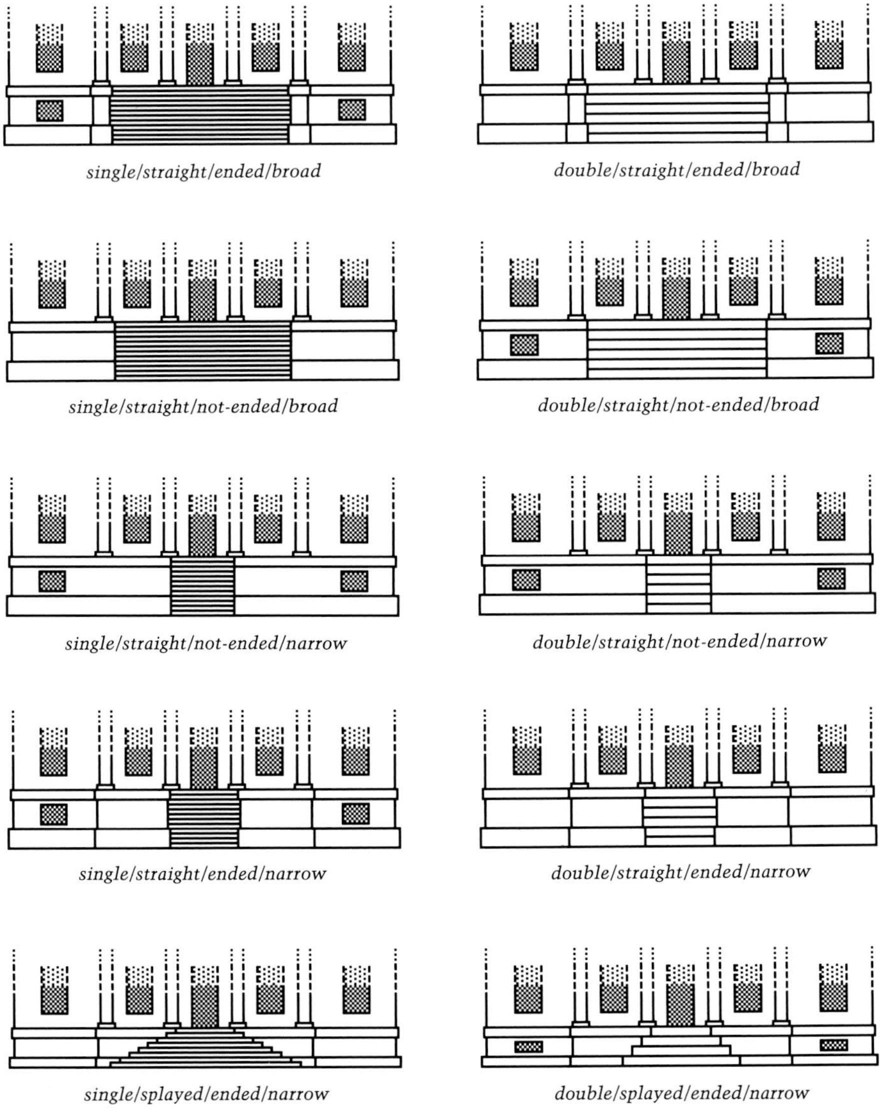

single/straight/ended/broad

double/straight/ended/broad

single/straight/not-ended/broad

double/straight/not-ended/broad

single/straight/not-ended/narrow

double/straight/not-ended/narrow

single/straight/ended/narrow

double/straight/ended/narrow

single/splayed/ended/narrow

double/splayed/ended/narrow

single/splayed/not-ended/narrow

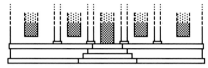

double/splayed/not-ended/narrow

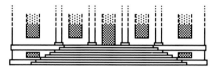

single/splayed/not-ended/broad

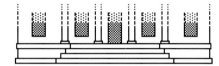

double/splayed/not-ended/broad

at Vicenza is similarly two stories and fully arcuated. He apparently considered this arrangement appropriate for grand civic structures and inappropriate for merely domestic ones. Therefore, we exclude it.

We also have purely stylistic reasons for striking the combinations in figures 3.16b and c. Although we followed Palladian proportions (which we will examine later) exactly in drawing these facades, in both of them the first and second stories differ substantially in height. Having both stories of equal height would not work because the taller arches would be spindly, while shorter columns would violate the rules governing the proportions of the classical orders. Additionally, in figure 3.16c a visually heavy floor teeters on slender supports, and the facade appears to have distended base-to-roof arches.

Palladio's facades do not correlate either the height or the shape of the roof with a particular body style. Similarly, no conventions govern base height or style. So we do not link the design of these two malleable blocks (base or roof) to any specific combinations.

Sixteen block combinations now remain. The five styles of floor block—columnar (column, column with dado, and colossal column), arcuated, and compositional—define the three major Palladian facade styles. The combinations we will

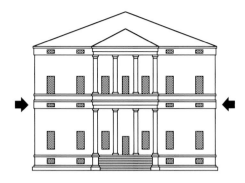

3.15 *A midfacade half entablature.*

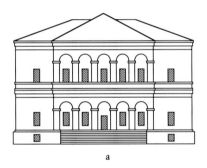

a

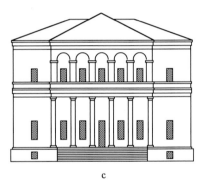

b   c

3.16 *Two-story arcuated facades.*

build on each of these constitute only the Palladian variations on these major themes; other reasonable but un-Palladian variations remain. Some combinations differ only slightly from others—substitution of a half entablature block for a full entablature block, for example—but each combination accommodates a wide variation of roof, base, door, and windows. Figure 3.17 illustrates an example of each combination as constructed by Facademaker using assorted permutations of doors, windows, roofs, and bases.

But we have yet to look at the connection between facade and plan that we cited earlier. As described so far, blocks are static objects, save for certain tightly defined variations, and function only as vertical components. To begin forging the plan-facade link, we contrast two villas. The Villa Emo (*Quattro Libri*, 2.55) and

3.17   *The sixteen facade styles (continues on following pages).*

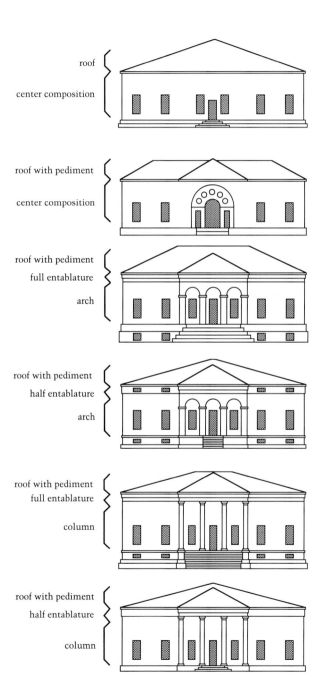

roof { }

center composition { }

roof with pediment { }

center composition { }

roof with pediment {
full entablature {

arch { }

roof with pediment {
half entablature {

arch { }

roof with pediment {
full entablature {

column { }

roof with pediment {
half entablature {

column { }

roof with pediment

attic
full entablature

arch

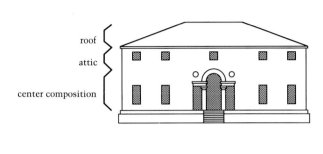

roof

attic

center composition

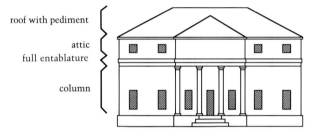

roof with pediment

attic
full entablature

column

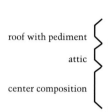

roof with pediment

attic

center composition

roof

attic
full entablature

arch

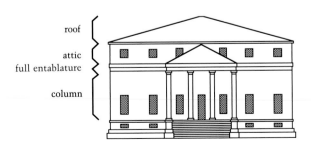

roof

attic
full entablature

column

roof with pediment

full entablature

colossal column

roof with pediment

half entablature

colossal column

roof with pediment

full entablature

column with dado

full entablature

column

roof with pediment

half entablature

column with dado

full entablature

column

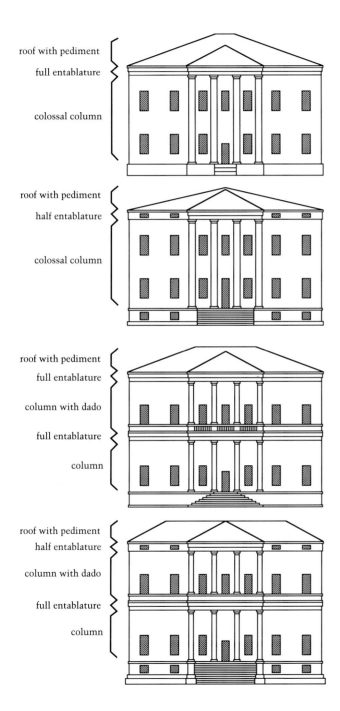

3.18 *Similar plans but different facades:*
the Villa Emo, Fanzolo (a), and the Villa
Pisani, Montagnana (b), both from the
Quattro Libri.

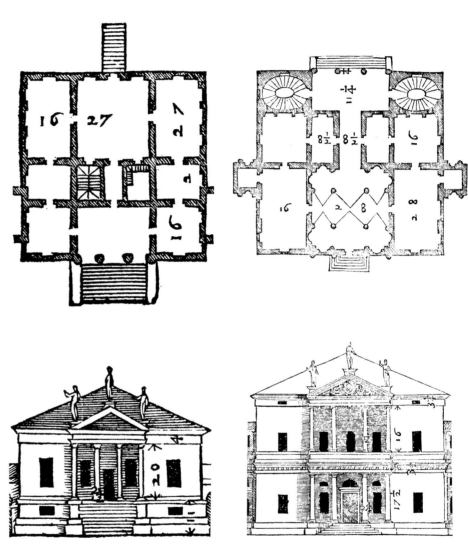

a

b

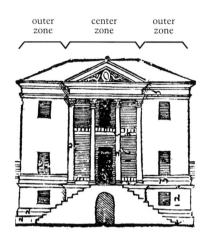

outer zone   center zone   outer zone

3.19   *Center and outer zones in the Villa Ragona, Ghizzolle di Montegaldella (Vicenza), from the* Quattro Libri.

the Villa Pisani (*Quattro Libri*, 2.52), illustrated in figure 3.18, are nearly mirror images in plan: nine-square in extent, with the center square divided into three spaces. Excluding wall widths, Emo measures 60 × 55 Vicentine feet, Pisani 59 × 55.

As illustrated by these examples, the facade has two distinct aspects. Its vertical aspect, or block combination in our language, is not linked to the plan, but its horizontal aspect most definitely is. Blocks are not static objects, for in width and latitudinal arrangement they are extremely fluid, and they can adjust in height as well. In order for facade to spring from plan, we must establish lines of communication between Facademaker and Planmaker—what things about the plan does Facademaker need to know? Or, paraphrasing Barbaro, precisely how is a tree born from its roots?

First, we define the terms "center zone" and "outer zone." As demonstrated on the Villa Ragona (fig. 3.19; *Quattro Libri*, 2.57), one can divide Palladio's facades into a center zone and two outer zones that are mirror reflections of each other. The center zone houses most facade details, such as columns, doors, arches, and pediments. Outer zones house only windows.

Palladio derives the center zone's width from the plan. Most often, he matches it to the width of the forward central room, as in the Palazzo Antonini (fig. 3.20a; *Quattro Libri*, 2.5). If that center zone proves too narrow for a minimum of four columns and three intercolumniations, then he expands it to equal the width of the widest room on the center axis, as in the Villa Cornaro (fig. 3.20b; *Quattro Libri*, 2.53). If this room is also too narrow, or should there be no wider room on the center axis, then he aligns the center zone with the three front center rooms, as in the Villa Angarano (fig. 3.20c; *Quattro Libri*, 2.63). The outer zones are simply those portions of the facade outside the center zone; in figure 3.20c there are no outer zones at all because the center zone is as wide as the entire plan.

Opposite design philosophies govern the two types of zone. Palladio determines placement of the outer zone's only detail, the window, by the plan. In figure 3.20, all the outer zone windows align with door axes in plan. But in the center zone (the

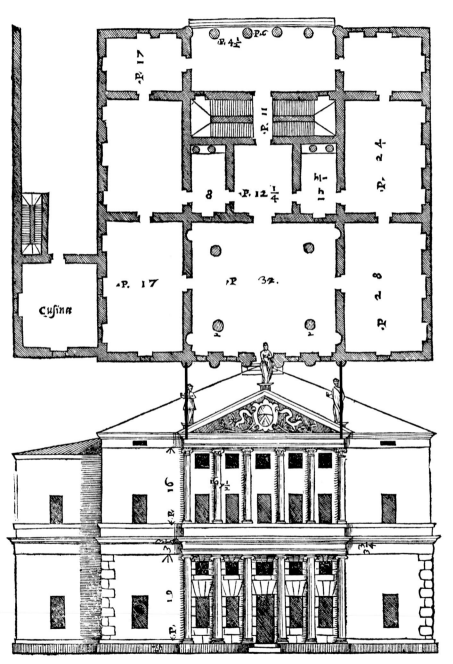

3.20 *Center zone widths in the Palazzo Antonini, Udine* (a); *the Villa Cornaro, Piombino Dese (Treviso)* (b); *and the Villa Angarano, Angarano* (c); *all from the Quattro Libri.*

a

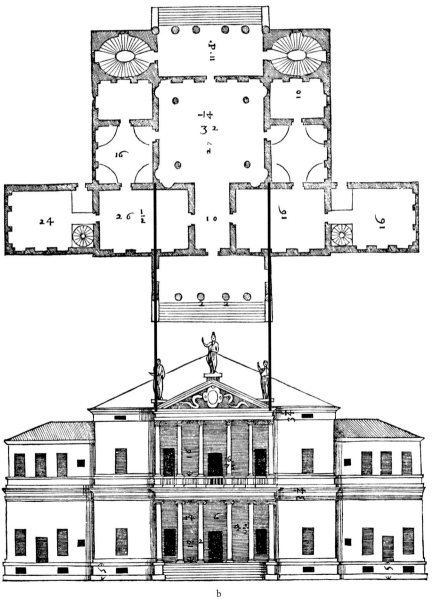

b

c

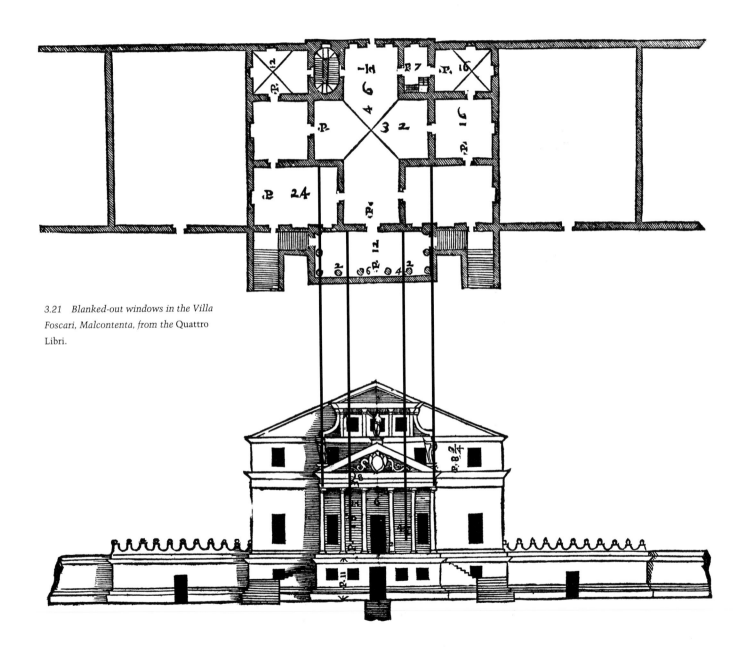

3.21 *Blanked-out windows in the Villa*
Foscari, Malcontenta, from the Quattro
Libri.

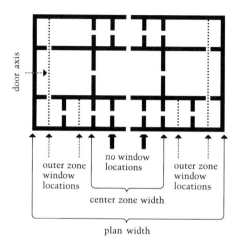

3.22 The four pieces of data passed from Planmaker to Facademaker.

land of abundant detail), facade overrules plan. There, window location is a by-product of column placement, which is in turn calculated by Palladian formulas. In this zone, ideal column spacing is everything; alignment of windows with the plan is nothing.

There is, however, a practical exception to the facade's hegemony in center zones. In the Villa Foscari (fig. 3.21; *Quattro Libri*, 2.50), the two windows that would normally flank the door are missing. Why? The center zone width and resulting column placement left those two windows squarely in front of two walls. Windows that open onto walls are an architectural absurdity, so Palladio simply erased such windows; note that he did not sacrifice or rearrange columns to solve this problem. There are thus traces of facade-plan conflict here.

Planmaker, then, passes to Facademaker the four pieces of information illustrated in the former's nearly completed plan in figure 3.22 (it lacks only windows). First is the plan's width; after all, plan and facade width must match. The second piece of data, center zone width, is calculated by Planmaker using Palladio's method illustrated in figure 3.20. (It need not pass outer zone width to Facademaker because this simply equals [plan width – center zone width] / 2.) Third is a list of outer zone window locations that Planmaker compiles from the vertical door axes running through outer zone rooms on the facade edge of the plan. Fourth and last are the wall locations within the center zone where Facademaker may not place windows.

In addition, we link the scale of plan and facade. As with Palladio, our unit of measurement throughout the facade is the column width. Following his usage in the *Quattro Libri*, our scale equates one wall width in plan to one column width in facade.

After receiving Planmaker's four nuggets of information and selecting one of the sixteen block combinations, Facademaker goes to work. It begins with body blocks, moving from bottom to top, and adds the base last. One of the five floor blocks—column, column with dado, arch, colossal column, or center composition—is laid out first. For all floor blocks except center composition blocks,

Facademaker determines first how many columns, colossal columns, or arch piers it can draw, then the height of each, and finally the dimensions of the windows. Only after making these calculations does it draw out the block.

For column and colossal column blocks, Facademaker bases its calculations on the proportions of Palladio's classical orders. He illustrates five orders in Book I—Tuscan, Doric, Ionic, Corinthian, and Composite—and for each enumerates the proper ratios for column height to column width and intercolumniation to column width. Facademaker cannot reproduce the orders, as our computer draws detail far less ably than a Renaissance engraver, but we can reflect the proportions of the various orders by fixing column width and varying column height and intercolumniation.

Colossal columns, which are twice the height of standard columns, and piers, which are the supporters of relatively heavy arches, ought to be wider than standard columns; we fix their widths at $1\frac{1}{3}$ column widths. We space columns more generously than Palladio to compensate for Facademaker's thick lines, but we do adhere to the classical principle of having columns grow taller and proportionally thinner as the intercolumniation decreases. Our ratios for column and colossal column blocks are shown numerically and graphically in figure 3.23.

Although Palladio offers no written instructions regarding arch proportions, his built instructions are relatively clear. There are five arcuated Palladian villas—Caldogno, Gazzotti, Pisani-Bagnolo, Saraceno, and Zeno—although only Saraceno is published as an arcuated facade in the *Quattro Libri*. The ratio of intercolumniation to pier width in these five varies between $1\frac{1}{2}{:}1$ and $2\frac{1}{2}{:}1$, but the proportion of the "springing box" in all is about 2:1. In other words, as the arch widens in span, the piers must grow taller to maintain the constant 2:1 ratio. As shown in figure 3.24, the relationship between intercolumniation and pier height is direct, and not inverse as with columns and colossal columns.

Depending on the type of floor block, Facademaker calculates the number of columns, colossal columns, or piers, depending on the block, that can fit within

Columns

column height :
column width

intercolumniation :
column width

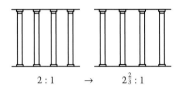

2 : 1 → $2\frac{2}{3}$: 1

$8\frac{2}{3}$: 1

3.23   Column spacing and height ratios.

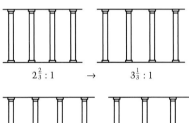

$2\frac{2}{3}$: 1 → $3\frac{1}{3}$: 1

8 : 1

$3\frac{1}{3}$: 1 → 4 : 1

$7\frac{1}{3}$: 1

Colossal columns

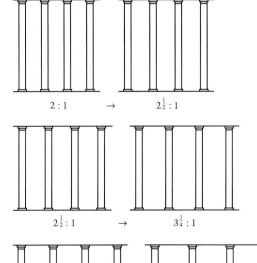

2 : 1 → $2\frac{1}{2}$: 1

11 : 1

$2\frac{1}{2}$: 1 → $3\frac{1}{4}$: 1

10 : 1

$3\frac{1}{4}$: 1 → 4 : 1

9 : 1

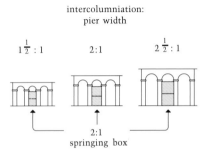

intercolumniation:
pier width

$1\frac{1}{2}:1$ $2:1$ $2\frac{1}{2}:1$

$2:1$
springing box

3.24 *Arch spacing and height ratios.*

the center zone. The intercolumniation must be somewhere between two and four widths for columns and colossal columns, or between $1\frac{1}{2}$ and $2\frac{1}{2}$ widths for piers. From the resulting intercolumniation, Facademaker calculates the proper height of the supports using the ratios from figures 3.23 and 3.24.

Next, Facademaker calculates window dimensions. Windows fall between columns. So, as intercolumniations narrow, window widths must do the same. To avoid a crush of numbers we will not list all the ratios of former to latter, but in general windows are roughly half as wide as intercolumniations. As the intercolumniation increases, however, this proportion diminishes. This is to prevent excessively wide windows. Palladio instructs us to make windows $2\frac{1}{6}$ as high as wide, and he follows this prescription closely in all his facades. So, as we adjust window width to a given intercolumniation, we also adjust window height to maintain this ratio. We illustrate progressive examples for column, colossal column, and arch blocks in figure 3.25.

In contrast to other floor blocks, center composition blocks do not adjust to center zone width. We store the different entrances from Palladio's center composition facades as fixed drawings. When laying out the block, Facademaker copies the chosen entrance from its library of drawings onto the facade.

In laying out floor blocks, then, we generate the facade from the plan. The width of the portico equals the width of the center zone as passed on from Planmaker. Indirectly, via Facademaker ratios, the center zone also determines the number and height of columns or arches, and the number and dimensions of windows. As to placement, Facademaker rules in the center zone, save for the matter of window-wall conflicts. But Planmaker rules in the outer zones. In sum, the horizontal as well as the vertical aspects of the facade do indeed spring from the plan.

We continue up the facade to the entablature. In his intended insert to Book I of the *Quattro Libri*, which did not appear at the time it was written but has recently been published (cf. our appendix), Palladio states that the entablature should be

Columns **Colossal columns** **Arches**

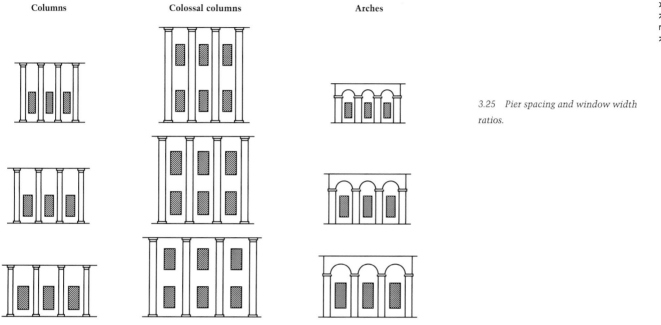

3.25   *Pier spacing and window width ratios.*

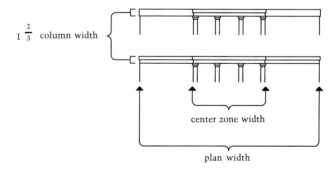

$1\frac{2}{3}$ column width

center zone width

plan width

3.26   *Entablature proportions.*

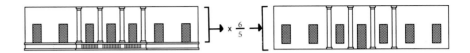

two column-widths high. In practice, however, entablatures in the *Quattro Libri* are closer to one and two-thirds column-widths. We follow practice instead of theory and fix the height of both half- and full-entablature blocks at one and two-thirds column-widths, as shown in figure 3.26. Both are slightly wider than the plan, so as just to overhang the facade body proper. Their center sections (or, in three dimensions, those portions protruding from the facade), are slightly narrower than the center zone and just short of the edges of their supporting capitals.

Although it is a type of floor block, we use the column with dado only as a second story in combination with a first-story column block. In locating second-story windows, we follow Palladio's instructions (which he states twice) to place the openings of doors and windows exactly over one another so that void may be over void and solid over solid. Similarly, Palladio tells us to place the upper columns directly above those underneath them (*Quattro Libri*, 1.6). Palladio's instructions regarding the height of the second story (see appendix) are also unambiguous: "the lower will have to be one-fifth higher than the upper one," to account for the effect of foreshortening. And, in fact, the first-story columns in the *Quattro Libri* are consistently $\frac{6}{5}$ the height of the second-story columns; practice does follow theory in this case. Nonetheless, if we include the dado when measuring the height of the second story, we find that the two stories are nearly the same height in all facades. So Facademaker shortens the second-story columns and inserts the dado, as illustrated in figure 3.27.

Palladio also tells us to use a lighter order on the second story than on the first, and he does so without fail both in the *Quattro Libri* and in his built villas. If the first story is Doric then the second story is Ionic; if the first is Ionic then the second is Corinthian. Since Facademaker does not distinguish between orders, we will simply have to imagine these differences.

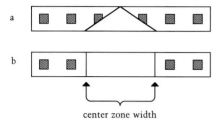

a

b

center zone width

3.28　Attic story proportions.

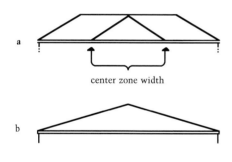

a

center zone width

b

3.29　Roof proportions.

The height of an attic block is one-third the height of its supporting floor block. In the attic with pediment, illustrated in figure 3.28a, pediment width equals center zone width, and pediment height equals that of the attic. The lines of the attic with center lines, shown in figure 3.28b, also define the edges of the center zone. As with column with dado blocks, all windows in attic blocks align with the windows of the first story, but adjust their height so as to remain square.

The facade capstone is the roof block. Both those with and those without pediment contain a narrow cornice that, like an entablature, is slightly wider than the facade body (fig. 3.29). Like attic pediments, roof pediments are as wide as the center zone. As related earlier, roof heights and shapes and roof pediment heights vary within limits based on the width of the facade.

Our system of facade construction is now complete, but Facademaker still has one remaining duty. The last element in the previous chapter, the windows, was not incorporated into the plan at the time because Planmaker knew neither the width nor the locations of the windows on the plan's facade edge. Both these decisions, we said, were to be up to Facademaker. Having now made these decisions, Facademaker can pass this information back to Planmaker.

So much for the villa's main facade. The other facades are easy. Although Facademaker draws neither rear nor side elevations, we, like Palladio, locate their windows according to the plan. In plan, Palladio's rear and side windows are the same width as the facade windows, and so Planmaker uses the same width for all windows.

Figure 3.30 illustrates how Planmaker cuts windows. On the facade edge of the plan, at each location indicated by Facademaker, Planmaker cuts a notch into the wall; the notch's width is equal to the window width relayed by Facademaker. On the plan's left and right edges it cuts the same notch at the end of each room's horizontal door axis. It does the same in each room on the top edge, cutting the notch at the end of the vertical door axis. As is appropriate to its humbler status, the rear facade resulting from this method is simpler than the front facade.

window width passed from Facademaker

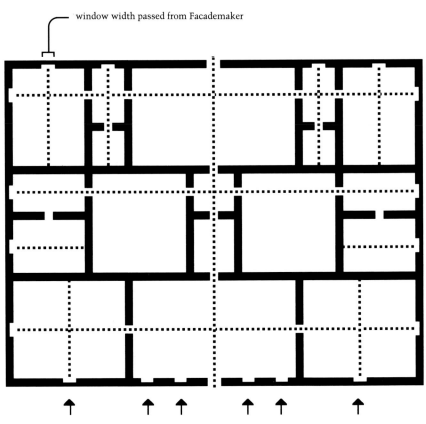

window locations passed from Facademaker

We have come full circle. Planmaker spoke to Facademaker and Facademaker spoke back. The fruit of their labor, a facade-plan combination such as could appear in the *Quattro Libri*, is illustrated in figure 3.31. We have drawn the rear and side facades manually to illustrate that one can build them using the same blocks from the front facade. Palladio's side facades are uniformly quite plain: he simply continues the cornices and stringcourses around from the front, and locates the windows according to plan. His rear facades, like that in figure 3.31, are more richly designed and often constitute a play on the main facade.[3]

Is our villa Palladian? We evaluate our method in the next chapter.

3.31   A sample villa.

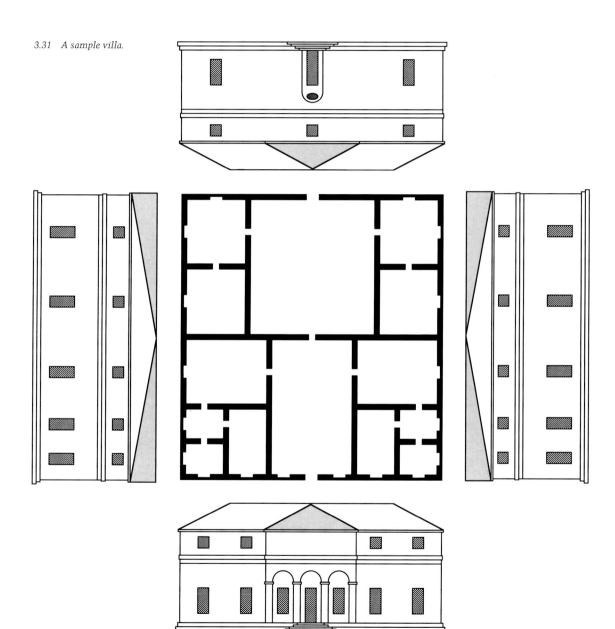

CONCLUSIONS

In the introduction we examined, and tentatively rejected, the idea that Palladio's plans are based on his canonical rectangles or on ratios derived from musical intervals. Let us look further at two aspects of this subject.

The first point regards the proportions of individual rooms. Planmaker has shown that Palladio's own list of canonical room proportions does not control his plan style. As to Planmaker itself, never in its splitting process does it check or adjust the proportions of a room except to ensure that it is less than two squares. It lets final room proportions lie where they fall, whether 1:1, 32:17, or 29:43. Yet, as we are about to see, Planmaker can nonetheless produce plans that an expert would not distinguish from Palladio's originals. Of course one might try to argue that our truly Palladian Planmaker designs are that way precisely because, by chance, they consist mostly or entirely of canonically shaped rooms. If Palladio had deployed his canon of shapes in a consistent way this would be a cogent argument. But in fact he does so haphazardly—just as Planmaker does, in fact.

Let us illustrate. In figure 4.1 are two plans, one the Villa Ragona from the *Quattro Libri* (minus doors, windows, and stairs, which allows us to focus solely on proportions), the other a plan we drew by hand. Can you tell which is the original? Actually, it's not possible: since Palladio uses his canon inconsistently, and since the only difference between the two plans lies in the shapes of the rooms, you cannot distinguish the actual from the imitation. To be truly "un-Palladian" means to break one of the rules we discovered in chapter 2, and neither of these plans does that.

Let's make the game easier. It has been said that Palladio labels dimensions in the *Quattro Libri* not simply to tell us the sizes of the rooms but to signal their proportions.[1] Palladio's dimensions, supposedly, serve a higher pedagogical purpose. Accordingly, in figure 4.2 we add the dimensions. We label them on the actual Villa Ragona exactly as Palladio does in the *Quattro Libri*, and we label our imitation similarly.

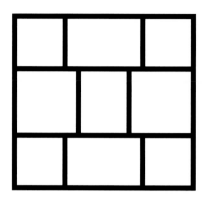

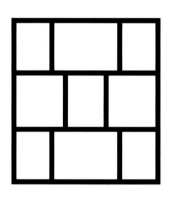

4.1   *Room shapes of a Palladian plan and of a hand-drawn imitation.*

But now that we have incorporated Palladio's proportional signals into the plan we have to note that plan *b*, which has *no* canonically shaped rooms, is the real Villa Ragona, and plan *a*, which has eight canonically shaped rooms out of nine, is the fake. So not only is the Villa Ragona completely noncanonical, Palladio has emphatically let us know this by inscribing the room dimensions on it. Our fake, furthermore, is only one of many simple ways he could have "perfected" his plan had he so desired. (One might argue that the 5:4 proportion found in each of Palladio's corner rooms is "harmonic" because 5:4 is a major third. But if Palladio considered 5:4 ideal, why didn't he include it in his canon?)

Another example. Figure 4.3a is the Villa Zeno, Donegal di Cessalto, from the *Quattro Libri*, and figure 4.3b is our "corrected" version. If Palladio were indeed intent on using canonical proportions, it is puzzling that he did not make the two minor adjustments we show, to wit: at point 1 we extend the plan's length by two feet, which makes the two 14×12 rooms into perfect squares; at points 2 and 3 we remove half a foot in width, which makes the ungainly $21\frac{1}{2} \times 14$ rooms each a canonical 21×14, or 3:2, while the top center room becomes a canonical 28×14, or 2:1. So our slight changes lead to a total of six newly canonical rooms. They also create a symphony of fourteens and multiples of fourteen that one supposes would appeal to Palladio. Why didn't he do something like this? One answer is variety—two adjacent rooms of the same size (14×14 in this case) are extremely rare in his work. But another answer is that he is much less doctrinaire than is commonly thought.

The second aspect of proportion that we want to discuss regards *sequences* of dimensions among rooms. These are what Wittkower refers to as Palladio's "fugal system of proportion."[2] One could assert that by having Planmaker use split ratios like 1:2 (an octave) and 3:2:3 (two perfect fifths) to create room sequences, we are in fact implementing a fugal system of proportions between neighboring rooms, and that that is why Planmaker works in the first place. However, Planmaker uses many nonmusical split ratios, like 3:1 and 4:1:4, and produces Palladian plans anyway. Also, even when using a musical ratio such as 3:2:3 there is only a slight

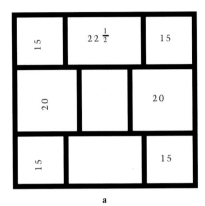

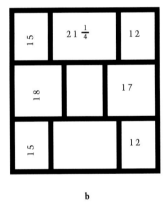

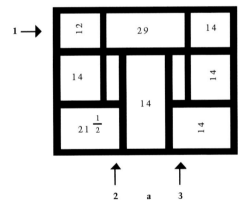

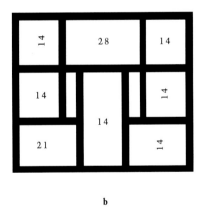

4.2 *Palladian plan and imitation, with dimensions labeled.*

4.3 *Dimensions in the Villa Zeno, Donegal di Cessalto (Treviso)* (a), *from the* Quattro Libri; *"corrected" version of the plan* (b).

chance that Planmaker will be able to split the room into a musical sequence. For example, if it splits a 50-foot-wide space using a 3:2:3 ratio, the resulting rooms will be a nonmusical sequence of 18, 14, and 18 feet wide, because 3:2:3 does not divide evenly into 50 but only into multiples of 8. One could also bring in our earlier argument: truly Palladian Planmaker plans are that way because, *purely by chance*, they incorporate musical sequences.

Many of Palladio's own plans contain dimensions that can never be massaged into a progression. The dimensions from the Villa Ragona (fig. 4.2b)—which has rooms that are 12, 15, 17, 18, and $21\frac{1}{4}$—and those from the Villa Zeno (fig. 4.3a)—with 12, 14, $21\frac{1}{2}$, and 29—fall into no known musical, harmonic, fugal, arithmetic, geometric, exponential, Fibonacci, or other sequence we know of. The conclusion is the same as for musical proportions within rooms: Palladio uses musical sequences but does so inconsistently. One therefore cannot formulate a theory of his style based on sequences.

It may be significant that Planmaker is equally averse to laying out consistent musical sequences. Early in our work we tried to teach it to do so, but the task proved impossible. First, we could not assemble a usable set of them. For example, Wittkower relates the dimensions from the Villa Pisani—16, 18, 24, and 32— using five different ratios, some musical, some canonical. But he gives no indication as to which type of ratio to use where, nor as to the order in which they are to occur. Secondly, sequences only cover some of the dimensions in any plan. What do we do about the others? Similar rogue dimensions are the 7 and $46\frac{1}{2}$ in Malcontenta (fig. 4.34). And thirdly, of course, there are the innumerable dimensions Palladio does not label. The order in which Planmaker could or should pick these stepchildren would have had a dramatic effect on any plan. Yet Wittkower's theory gives us no guidance as to how to do so. What we need, instead, are the rules painstakingly discovered above in chapter 2.

Finally, a reply to those who have argued that one should use a shape grammar to generate plans consisting only of square rooms, and that one can worry about proportion later. This would mean that we would learn nothing about the actual

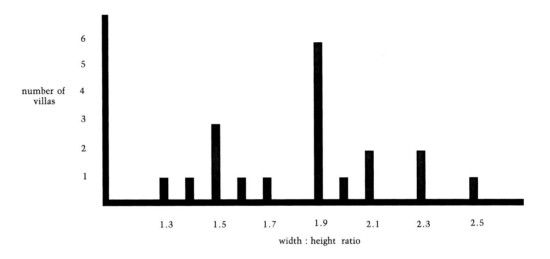

4.4 Distribution of facade width/height ratios for villas in the Quattro Libri.

role of proportion in Palladio—which, as we have just seen, is, despite its inconsistent occurrence, an all-important subject. By empowering Planmaker to generate proportions at random we have discovered the exact limits of that role. A shape grammar would not have taught us that Palladio's proportional system is much less rigid, much less central, than previously thought, that musical and other ideal ratios don't hurt but don't by themselves determine Palladian qualities.

Palladio's facades make the same point. Aside from remaining within certain bounds, they too conform to no rigid proportional rules. To show this, we have calculated the width/height ratio for all the villa facades in the *Quattro Libri* and plotted them on the bar graph in figure 4.4. What the chart shows us is that Palladio preferred facade width-to-height ratios of about 2:1 but used others as he saw fit. Reflecting this fact, our system accordingly has no fixed proportional link between plan width and facade height except for the constraints imposed by a few pieces of data that Planmaker passes to Facademaker (see chapter 3). This insouciance exactly matches the master's.

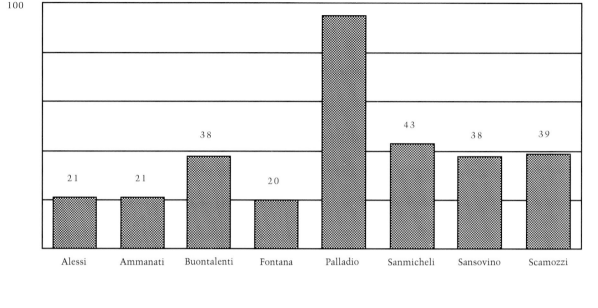

4.5 *The built output of selected Renais-*
sance architects.

Using a noncomputerized version of this method, furthermore, Palladio would have been able to design a building fairly rapidly. The method's flexibility, indeed, was probably one thing that made it possible for him to design large numbers of unique buildings—in other words, to be "paradigmatic." We should therefore not be surprised that he was prolific. Between 1531 and 1580 he was responsible for no less than 143 projects and buildings, not to mention scores of drawings, illustrations for Barbaro's Vitruvius, and the *Quattro Libri*. This comes out to an average of three built buildings a year.[3] Given the technology of the time, the remoteness of many of the sites, and the complexity of some of his large urban projects, Palladio's output is considerable. We believe that this productivity is in part, at least, the result of his efficient system of laying out plans and facades.

To buttress the point we turned to the *Macmillan Dictionary of Architects*, which lists a total of eight Italian architects more or less contemporary with Palladio who each produced 20 buildings or more (fig. 4.5). (The *Dictionary* credits Palladio with only 95 structures rather than the 143 in Puppi's catalogue; it does not count small jobs, altars, doorways, and the like.) The difference among the architects is striking: Palladio's productivity is more than double that of his next most productive rival, Michele Sanmicheli, and triple or quadruple that of everyone else.

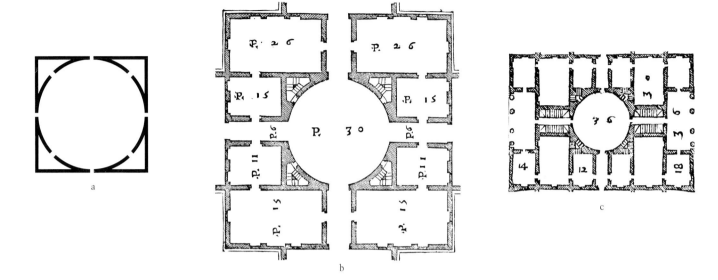

4.6 *Rotundas in plan: archetypal (*a)*; the Villa Rotonda, Vicenza (*b)*, from the* Quattro Libri; *the Villa Trissino, Meledo di Sarego (Vicenza) (*c)*, from the* Quattro Libri.

The method we have described works well for most types of Palladian villa, but there are other designs by Palladio that it could never produce. Let us look at a few of them: the experience may help whoever wants to continue with our project. More important, it will give us further insights into Palladio's mind.

First of all, Planmaker cannot produce circular rooms as in the Rotonda (fig. 4.6b). To correct this failing, we could of course tell the program to inscribe a circle every so often in one of the square rooms it so frequently produces. We could then get circular rotundas with four identical residual rooms as in figure 4.6a, as in the Rotonda itself, or as in the Villa Trissino (fig. 4.6c). But unfortunately there is more to it. Figures 4.6b and c illustrate the only two circular rooms in all Palladio's published domestic plans. In both schemes the rotundas must sit precisely in the center of the whole. To extrapolate a rule from these two examples, we would have to allow Planmaker to inscribe a circle in a square only when the square is central and the plan symmetrical on both the *x* and *y* axes. Theoretically Planmaker can produce such plans, but statistically the chances of its doing so are nearly zero. Anyway, this type of plan, we have just seen, is a rarity in Palladio's own domestic oeuvre. We can set it down as a "sport," an interpolation from public and urban architecture.

Similarly, Planmaker is at present unable to design T, I, and Greek cross–shaped rooms; and these shapes are not rarities in Palladio. Given our present technique, the only way to create them is to erase some of the walls in an all-rectangle plan. All of Palladio's nonrectangular rooms are in fact just such derivations from rectangular spaces; he himself erases walls, so to speak. The Villa Pisani at Montagnana (fig. 3.18b) and a study for the Villa Gazzotti (fig. 4.26) are typical. (The facade we generated for this latter building, by the way, is extremely close to what was built.)

But, again, there is more to it. Look at two of Palladio's most memorable nonrectangular spaces, the Greek crosses of the villas Barbaro and Malcontenta (figs. 4.22, 4.34). Carving out crosses like these from completed plans is difficult and would require a Planmaker much cleverer than ours. Furthermore, Palladio seems to have developed his plans *from* the crosses, while Planmaker always does the reverse and starts with the building's envelope. It would therefore have to carve its crosses out of whatever central set of symmetrical rectangles it ended up with. This is no minor computational task. On the other hand a new or alternative Planmaker, specifically for central-plan houses, is certainly a possibility.

Palladio's facades are also less tersely defined than we have implied. Some do not conform to our horizontal structure of a center zone and two outer ones. Others conform horizontally but cannot be modeled vertically as stacks of discrete blocks.

Figure 4.7a, a drawing in the Royal Institute of British Architects, London, thought to be either for the Villa Valmarana at Vigardolo or for that of Taddeo Gazoto at Bertesina, is what in our system we have called a simple base + center composition + roof facade. (If, as is thought, the villa was designed for two families, Palladio would purposely have replaced the normal single center focus with this pair of flanking foci.) To accommodate such a design to our system, we

4.7 *Unusual facades: a drawing possibly for the Villa Valmarana, Vigardolo di Monticello (a), from the British Architectural Library, RIBA, London, Palladio XVII, 15r; the Villa Thiene di Villafranca Padovana, Cicogna (b), from the* Quattro Libri.

a

b

could easily divide the facade into our standard center zone plus two outer ones. But our current rules would still force the main emphasis onto the center rather than the two ends as in the drawing. The "center composition block," a prime part of Facademaker's procedure, is simply not present in Palladio's scheme. Facademaker, furthermore, draws only rectangular windows in the outer zones, and here the outer zones have serlianas. The roof block, meanwhile, unlike those created by Facademaker, has not one pediment but three.[4]

On the other hand, in the Villa Thiene, Cicogna (fig. 4.7b), Palladio does not redefine the zones but does append a second pair of outer zones. The facade area between the towers is perfectly producible by our system. And our system could also produce two pairs of outer zones. However, whatever outermost pairs it produced could never consist of separate horizontal groupings each with distinct rooflines yet without entablatures, as here.

4.8   *The Villa Poiana, Poiana Maggiore.*

4.9   *The Villa Sarego, Verona (a), photo Scala/Art Resource; a drawing of the Villa Pisani, Bagnolo di Lonigo (b), from the British Architectural Library, RIBA, London, Palladio XVII, 17r.*

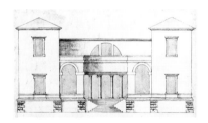

b

a

The project for the Villa Poiana (fig. 4.8) also defies our method—not horizontally this time but vertically. It cannot be analyzed into blocks because the entrance arch has deeply invaded the attic block. Our system has to separate facades into discrete, consistently horizontal bands, and we note that nearly all of Palladio's other villa facades are treated in just this way. In this sense Poiana is the exception that proves the rule.

Other facades go beyond our present possibilities in other ways. The Villa Sarego (fig. 4.9a) is zoneless, according to our system, because its U-shaped portico has no defined center aside from the front door. Figure 4.9b, a drawing for the Villa Pisani at Bagnolo, is also unusual. Horizontal and vertical elements overlap on several layers. Palladio even has a colonnade side by side with flanking arches, which is common enough in the work of his contemporaries but unique among the villas we are considering.

The anomalies analyzed above involve one-of-a-kind specimens, so our failure to encompass them is not crucial. But our system does have a number of other foibles that are thoroughly generic to it. A more complicated program (taking up a huge amount of memory) could eliminate most of these generic foibles. For now we will content ourselves with simply pointing them out; we will hold the virtues of simplicity superior to those of completeness. (One problem with a too-perfect program, aside from its inordinate length, is that it would soon begin to narrow the options down to Palladio's actual schemes. Its idea of what Palladio *would* do would turn quickly into what he *did* do, and nothing more.)

We will illustrate Planmaker's foibles in decreasing degrees of "un-Palladianness." The first few, indeed, are blatantly un-Palladian and could and should eventually be programmed out of existence. The later foibles imitate what Palladio himself did when, as happened, he broke his own rules. We should reemphasize that what follows applies only to villa planning, not palazzo planning. Most of the following "flaws"—for example, having a large number of room layers—are perfectly acceptable in city palaces.

First, the plans in figure 4.10 suffer from varying degrees of what we call checkerboarding. These are plans with too many rooms, especially too many interior rooms. None of Palladio's own villas has more than twenty rooms or more than four interior rooms, including staircases. Some of our plans exceed these limits. Obviously this is the result of too much splitting and aligning. Although some of Palladio's own plans do approach checkerboarding, he never designs unadulterated grids like those in figure 4.11. There is always at least one internal break or variation. The plans in figure 4.12, on the other hand, while they exceed Palladio's limit as to the number of internal rooms and the number of rooms in general, are not checkerboards and so are relatively inoffensive. An obvious though somewhat clumsy solution would have Planmaker count the number of rooms as it went along. Then, when it came to the limit, it would simply stop splitting and draw out whatever it had done up to that point.

Another problem is Planmaker's penchant for creating narrow rooms along the vertical center string. The largest room in every Palladian villa is not necessarily right in the middle of the plan, but it does always lie on this vertical axis. Therefore in the two plans in figure 4.13 the central vertical string is too narrow. As a result, even if Planmaker had not split the center rooms at all there would still be no room for a large central hall. In a related foible, the plans in figure 4.14 have center vertical strings wide enough to accommodate a large central hall, yet the largest rooms in both plans are on the flanks. This is a clear violation.

A third problem is that Planmaker can make plans with too many layers of rooms. We will define the number of horizontal or vertical layers in a plan as the greatest number of rooms intersected by any line drawn perpendicularly through the plan. For example, figure 4.15a has nine vertical layers and figure 4.15b seven. Palladio's villa plans never have more than four. Given Planmaker's proclivities, a plan with more than seven such layers would probably also have too many rooms. There are exceptions: figure 4.15c has an acceptable seventeen rooms but nine horizontal layers.

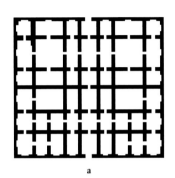 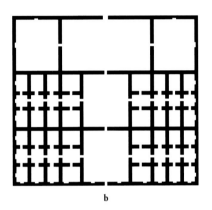 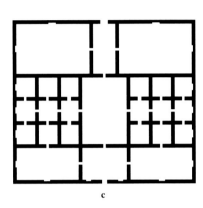

a   b   c

4.10   Bad plans 1: checkerboards.

4.11   Bad plans 2: monotonous grids.

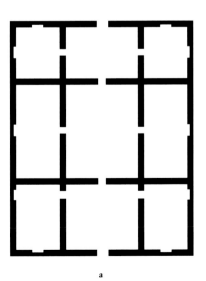 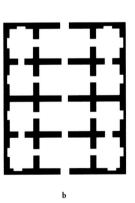

a   b

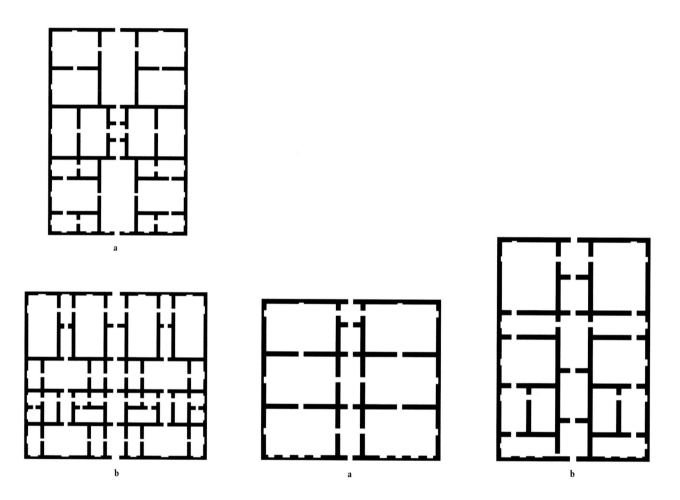

4.12   Bad plans 3: too many rooms.

4.13   Bad plans 4: center string too narrow.

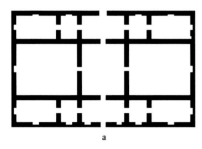

a

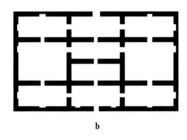

b

4.14 *Bad plans 5: center court too small.*

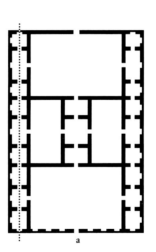

a

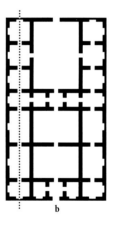

b

4.15 *Bad plans 6: too many layers.*

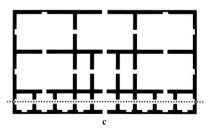

c

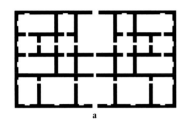

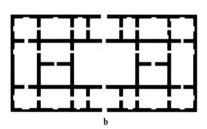

There is also the problem of extra interior rooms. As stated earlier, Palladio's villas never have more than four, even counting staircases. Overall, the plans in figure 4.16 do not have too many rooms. Nor do they have *far* too many interior rooms, as the checkerboard plans usually do; but they do have *a few* too many—seven in figure 4.16a and five in figure 4.16b.

Another foible might be called disparate room scale. Palladio tells us explicitly that center halls are supposed to be the largest rooms in the plan. The plans themselves tell us that the disparity between the largest and the smallest rooms should not be too great. Even if we consider small staircase halls as rooms, Palladio's most extreme ratio is 9:1. To our eyes, both plans in figure 4.17 seem misproportioned because they have largest-to-smallest room ratios of about 14:1.

4.16 *Bad plans 7: too many interior rooms.*

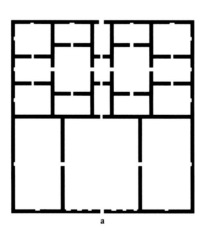

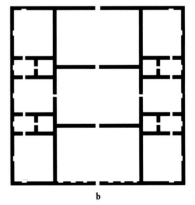

4.17 *Bad plans 8: disparate room scale.*

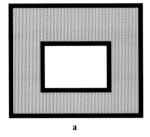

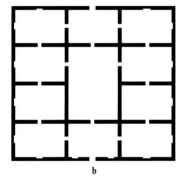

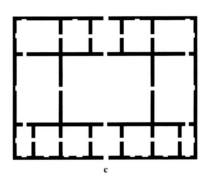

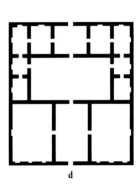

4.18 Good plans 1: doughnuts.

THE TRIUMPHS OF PLANMAKER AND FACADEMAKER

We have seen that, despite its several foibles and occasional outright failures, Planmaker is nonetheless capable of true Palladianism. Let us now look further at some of these triumphs.

A first group of designs consists of what we will call doughnut plans. These follow the basic form of figure 4.18a, consisting of a single layer of rooms around a central hall (figs. 4.18b–d). Palladio uses this simple doughnut arrangement occasionally, most notably in the Villa Rotonda (fig. 4.6b). The Villa Cornaro (fig. 3.20b) is another such. A second basic Palladian type is the upside-down U shown in figure 4.19a. Figures 4.19b and c have the same configuration, as do built villas like Angarano (fig. 3.20c). Most often, however, Palladio's plans are neither pure

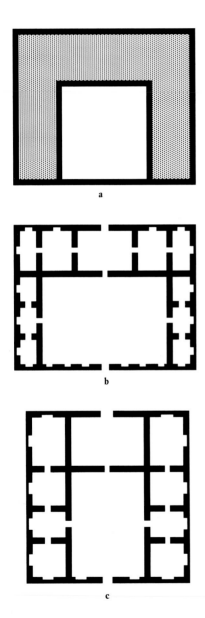

a

b

c

4.19 *Good plans 2: upside-down U's.*

doughnut nor pure U but variations on these shapes. The Villa Valmarana at Lisiera (fig. 2.3a) and figures 4.20a and b are thus quasi doughnuts, since the outer layer is not always one room deep. Similarly the plans in figures 4.20c and d, as well as the Villa Zeno (fig. 2.16a), are what we might call partially multilayered U's.

The designs shown so far have no close counterparts in Palladio's oeuvre. In other cases, with no prompting on our part and purely by virtue of their own internal rules, Planmaker and Facademaker created close approximations of actual villas by Palladio. In the following pages we will set designs by Planmaker and Facademaker next to their closest Palladian cousins. (We have felt free to remove walls manually from some of our plans in order to create nonrectangular spaces, e.g., Greek crosses. Where we have made these manual alterations we illustrate the computer's original in the center and the altered version on the right.)

In the Villa Angarano, to take one example (fig. 4.21), the five small rooms surrounding the top of the center hall are all an "imperfect" 18×13 feet. In Planmaker's version they are perfect squares. Unlike Palladio's center hall, Planmaker's is not a perfect 2:1 rectangle, but you can't see the difference without measuring. The facades of the two villas also teach an interesting lesson. The Villa Angarano has four columns and the computer's facade six. In this case Facademaker is being more "Palladian" than Palladio. Palladio tells us that his columns are 4 feet in diameter, and from the plan we know they are 18 feet apart. So the intercolumniation ratio is 18:4, or 4.5:1. This is considerably greater than Palladio's own prescribed 2:1 ratio for the Corinthian order. But, by using only four columns, Palladio was able to locate the outer zone windows on the facade so that in plan they line up on axis. Facademaker on the other hand played by the rules: it used a ratio of 2.5:1, and so had to insert two more columns. Consequently, its windows are off-axis. In short, Palladio knew when to break his own rules.

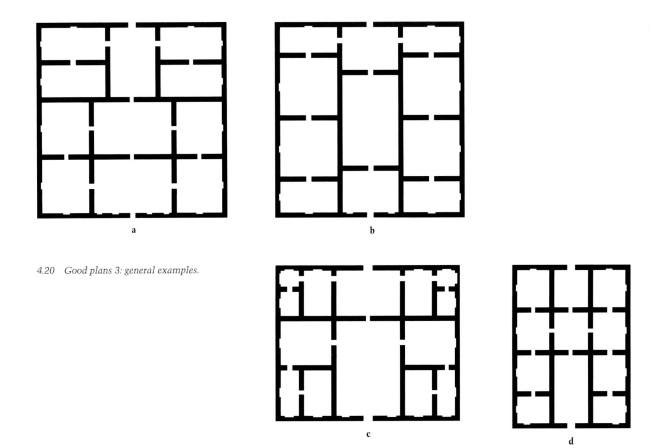

4.20 *Good plans 3: general examples.*

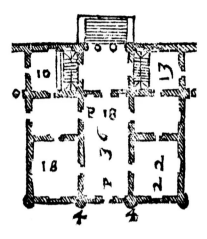
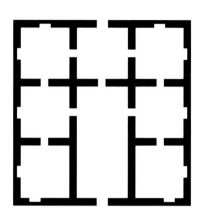

4.21   *The Villa Angarano, Angarano (Basso della Grappa), from the* Quattro Libri.

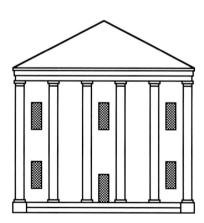

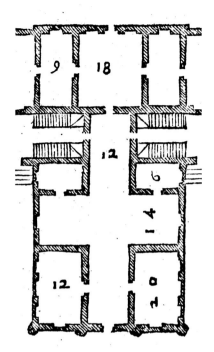

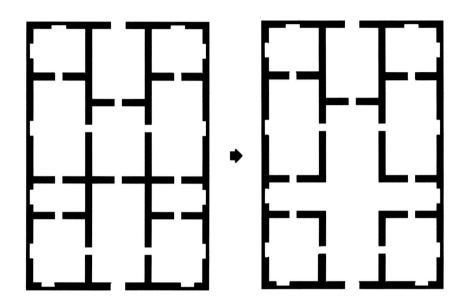

4.22   *The Villa Barbaro, Maser, from the* Quattro Libri. *The column-spacing lesson of the Villa Angarano applies here as well.*

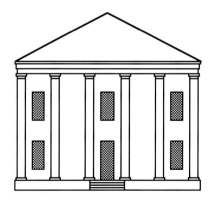

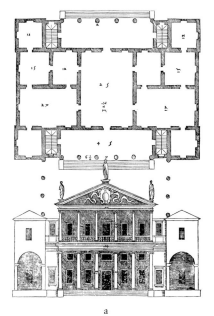

a

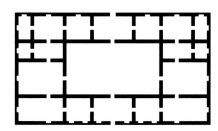

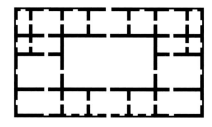

b

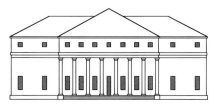

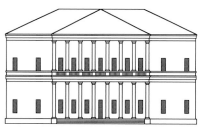

c

4.23 *The Villa Valmarana, Lisiera da Balzano Vicentino, from the* Quattro Libri. *Like the Villa Thiene, the Villa Valmarana has two outer zones. We have not been able to recreate its* Quattro Libri *facade precisely; figure* b *is Facademaker's best attempt. In figure* c *Facademaker does better in its recreation of the facade as it was actually built (see figure 3.6c).*

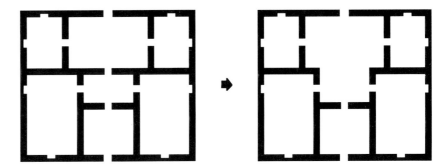

4.24   *The Villa Saraceno, Finale di Agugliaro, from the* Quattro Libri.

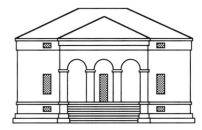

4.25 *The Villa Mocenigo, Marocco, from the* Quattro Libri.

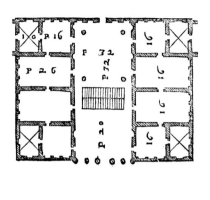

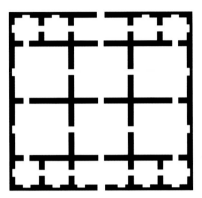

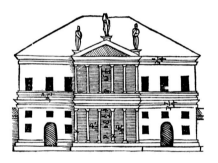

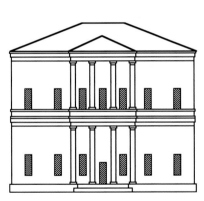

4.26   The Villa Gazzotti, Bertesina (Vicenza), drawings from the British Architectural Library, RIBA, London (facade, Palladio XVII, 27r; plan, Palladio XVI, 18r). One could consider the computer's unpilastered facade a minimalist interpretation of the original.

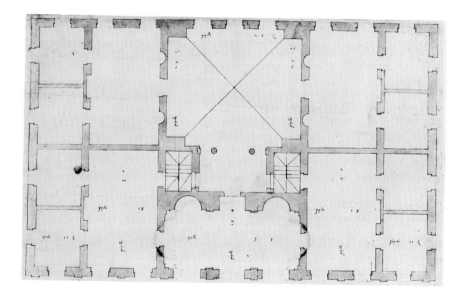

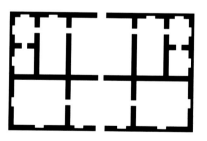

4.27   *The Villa Cornaro, Piombino Dese* *(Treviso), from the* Quattro Libri.

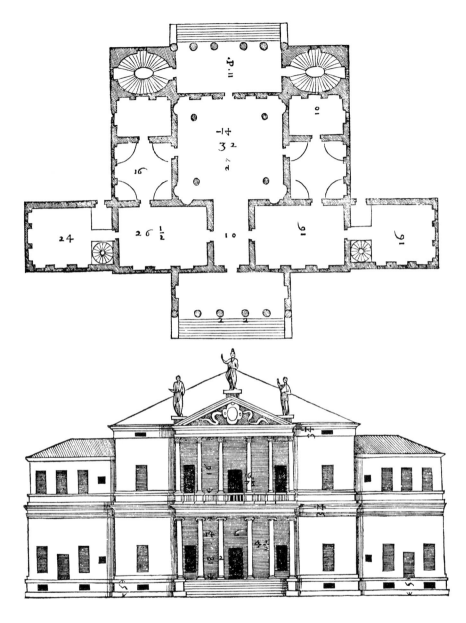

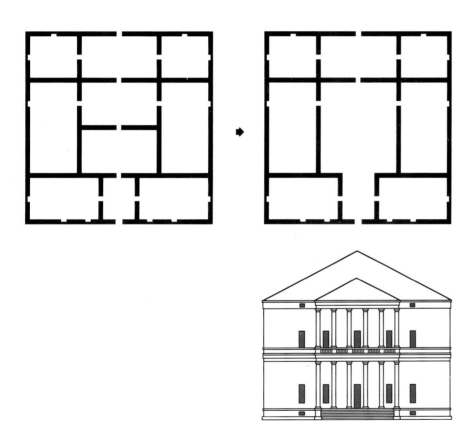

4.28 *The Villa Badoer, Fratta Polesine*
(Rovigo), from the Quattro Libri.

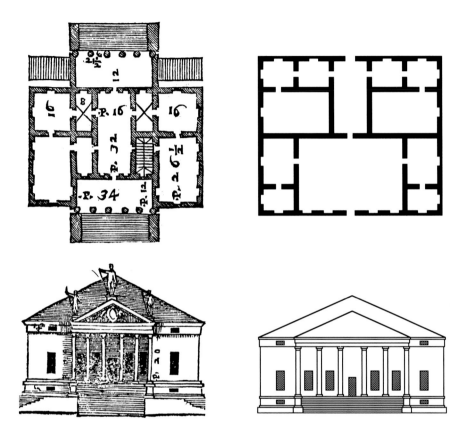

4.29 *The Villa Zeno, Donegal di Cessalto (Treviso), from the* Quattro Libri *and as built (photograph by Philip Trager, reproduced from Trager,* The Villas of Palladio*). Facademaker does not do thermal windows, but we note that in the actual built villa Palladio did not use them either.*

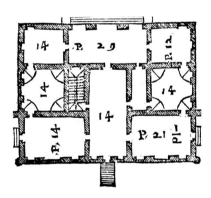

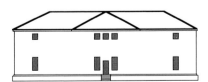

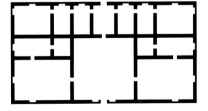

4.30   The Palazzo Della Torre, Verona,
from the Quattro Libri.

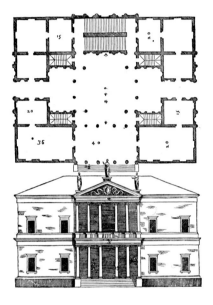

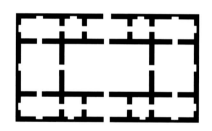 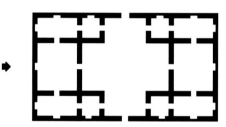

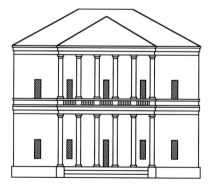

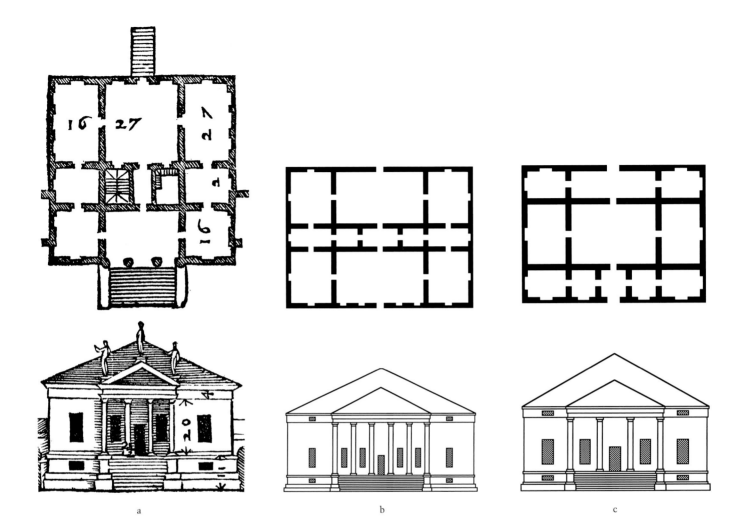

a

b

c

4.31　The Villa Emo, Fanzolo (Treviso),
from the Quattro Libri. *Facademaker's
center zone is slightly wider than
Palladio's, so six columns fit instead of
four (a, b). In variation* c, *Planmaker has
shifted the triple division from the center
to the front.*

4.32 The Palazzo Antonini, Udine, from the Quattro Libri. *Here Planmaker has further subdivided the center rooms, transforming the plan of the Villa Emo into that of the Villa-like Palazzo Antonini.*

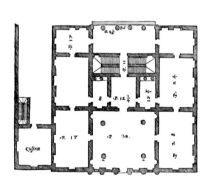

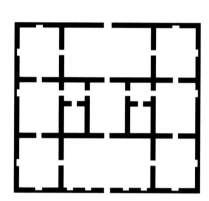

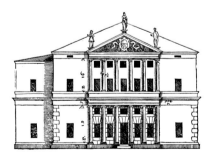

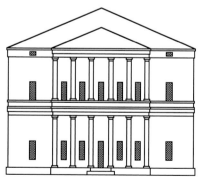

4.33   The Villa Valmarana, Vigardolo di Monticello, drawing from the British Architectural Library, RIBA, London, Palladio XVII, 2r. This is another close variation of the Villa Emo plan. Facademaker has approximated both the facade on the project drawing and the facade as built (compare figure 3.4c).

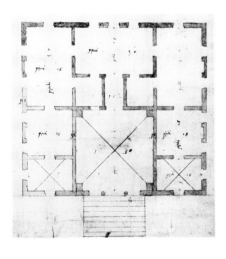

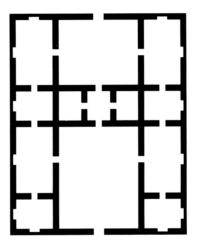

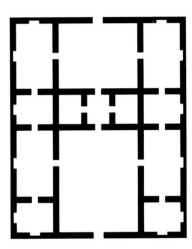

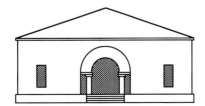

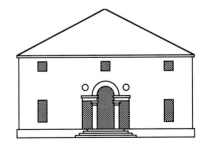

4.34 The Villa Foscari, Malcontenta, from
the Quattro Libri.

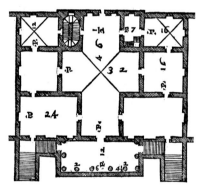

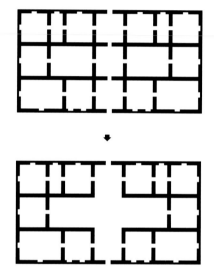

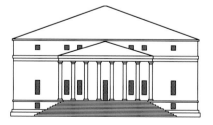

4.35   *The Villa Ragona, Ghizzolle di Montegaldella, Vicenza, from the* Quattro Libri.

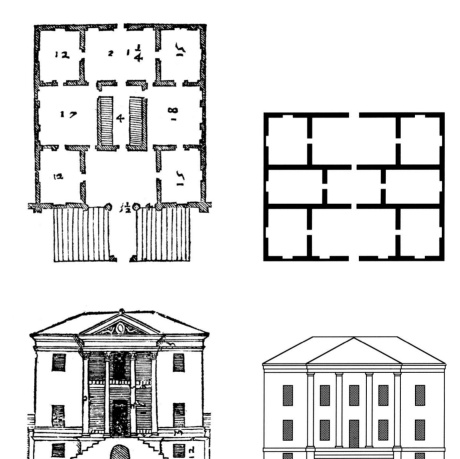

The Palladian villa, especially as published in the *Quattro Libri*, was an essential model for later Venetian architects, chief among them Vincenzo Scamozzi. Farther afield, Palladio's ideas deeply influenced the work of Lord Burlington, William Kent, and James Gibbs in England and that of Thomas Jefferson in America. Palladian ideas have marched on down to the present. Colin Rowe has shown that striking parallels exist, for example, between the plans of Palladio's Villa Malcontenta and Le Corbusier's Villa Stein.[5]

One virtue of our rules is that, in a more systematic and convincing way than hitherto, they can be used to separate Palladio's own work from that of his host of imitators. Let us begin with Palladio's closest follower, Scamozzi. In his plan for the Pisani villa at Rocca Pisana presso Lonigo (fig. 4.37), the building is contained in roughly a 60-foot square. A central dome is set into a square base exactly one quarter the size of the outer square. So far the building is strongly reminiscent of Palladio's Rotonda (fig. 4.36). But instead of rotating an L of rooms at 90° intervals around the dome core, as Palladio does in both his domed villas, Scamozzi's scheme makes use of Palladio's own more characteristic system: he has a central vertical string of spaces with symmetrical flanking sides. Here is a triple vertical split with a ratio of 1:2:1, which establishes the two outer sections, and then a central string containing the dome. The horizontal split meanwhile is 2:1:1:3. In short Scamozzi here puts together two Palladian systems, strings on the one hand, rotated L's on the other, that Palladio himself kept distinct. Nevertheless the result is close to being in accord with our rules. And the facade, except for the octagonal drum, is also something that our software might easily produce.

Yet Scamozzi did not always remain so tightly tethered to his master's rules. His plan for the Villa Molini, near Padua (fig. 4.38), is a standard Palladian doughnut but has an asymmetrical stair. In the facade there is what we would call a perfect half entablature block, plus a column with dado block that is on top of a center composition block. But Palladio never seems to have designed a belvedere of the type we see here. Scamozzi also departs from Palladio in his project for a villa on

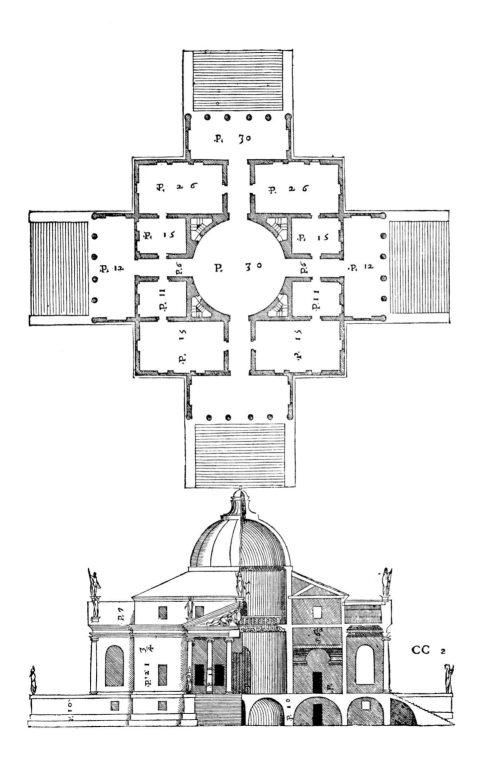

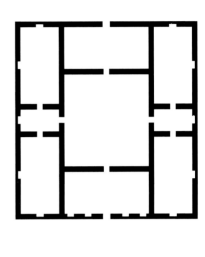

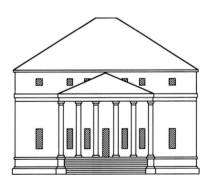

4.36 The Villa Rotonda, Vicenza, from the Quattro Libri. *This is the computer's best equivalent of the most famous of all of Palladio's villas. The dome could not be reproduced, as Facademaker does only pitched roofs.*

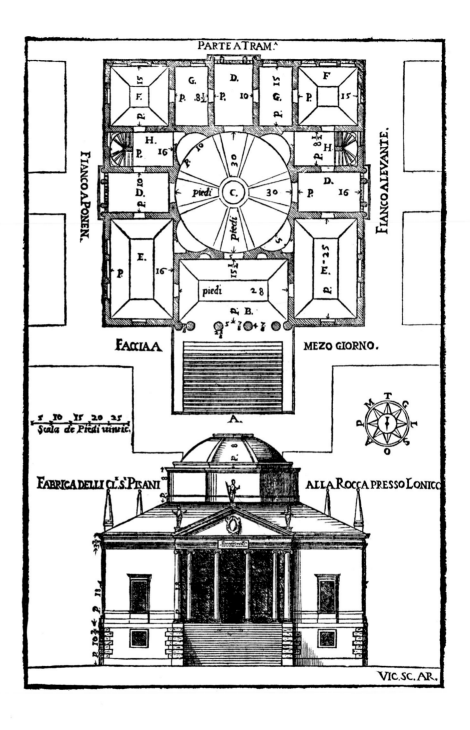

4.37 *Vincenzo Scamozzi, Villa Pisani, Rocca Pisana, from Scamozzi's* Idea della Architettura universale.

4.38   *Vincenzo Scamozzi, Villa Molini,*
from Scamozzi's Idea della Architettura
universale.

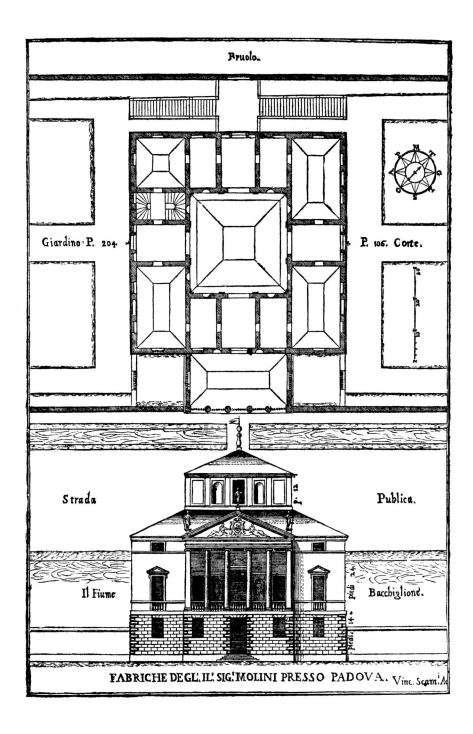

Bruolo.

Giardino· P. 204

P. 106. Corte.

Strada

Publica.

Il Fiume

Bacchiglione.

FABRICHE DE GL'. IL'. SIG'. MOLINI PRESSO PADOVA. Vinc. Scam'. Ae

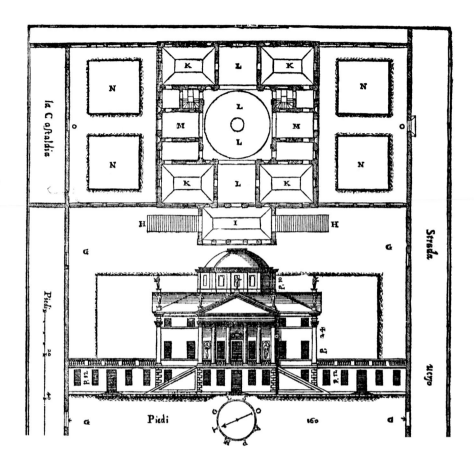

4.39 Vincenzo Scamozzi, project for a suburban villa on the Brenta, from Scamozzi's Idea della Architettura universale.

4.40 John Webb, design for the south front of Wilton House, from Colen Campbell, Vitruvius Britannicus (1715ff.). Courtesy RIBA.

the Brenta (fig. 4.39). The plan follows Palladio's rules to the letter except that the central hall is about thirteen times larger than the small rooms adjacent to the stairs. This un-Palladian disparity is even greater if we consider the whole central string as a single room of Greek cross shape. On the facade, meanwhile, the third-story windows bleed down into the column block. Though there are a few Palladio facades that, similarly, are not composed of truly discrete sections, none of them uses the arrangement Scamozzi has chosen here.

Indeed for Scamozzi even such a basic Palladian necessity as the rectangular perimeter was not particularly normative. He has many T-shaped plans. And, though he often worked on a larger scale than Palladio, he preferred not to use the colossal orders Palladio loved. Instead, he favored individual superimposed colonnades or pilastrades for each floor. In fact only a small proportion of the designs in Palladio's repertory fully overlap, in terms of our rules, with Scamozzi's most characteristic work.

The most important center of Palladianism outside Italy was probably Great Britain. During the seventeenth and eighteenth centuries a whole series of classical country houses was erected, most of them, then and now, described as "Palladian." One of the earliest is by Inigo Jones's assistant John Webb. A glance at Webb's design for the famous south front of Wilton House, near Salisbury (c. 1649; fig. 4.40),[6] however, shows that the whole shape by our standards is far too long and low. The Baroque central stair with its four differently oriented flights is equally anomalous. Palladio's only remotely comparable design is that for the Villa Pisani at Bagnolo (*Quattro Libri*, 2.47), which has lateral towers and an arched frontispiece. Other examples could be mentioned. But Palladio does not integrate towers with pedimented tops into the facade plane, as happens at Wilton, and he certainly never starts a story, as at either end of Webb's facade, and then fails to continue that story across. Finally, he never designs a frontispiece that is so small by comparison with the facade as a whole.

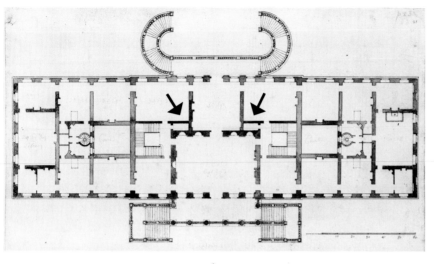

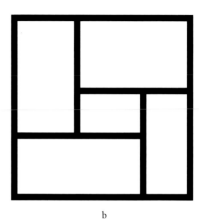

a   b

4.41   *Colen Campbell, plan for Wanstead I*
(a), from Vitruvius Britannicus, *courtesy*
RIBA; a spiral (b).

Another instructive design is Colen Campbell's 1715 plan for Wanstead I (fig. 4.41a). Here, first of all, there is an un-Palladian disparity between the largest and the smallest room (about 15:1). Another, more obvious departure is in the areas of the plan indicated by the arrows (added by us). This arrangement of rooms we call a spiral cluster (fig. 4.41b). Why might such a device interest an architect? For one thing, spiral clusters are the only way to divide a given rectangle into smaller ones without splitting. (Notice that no wall in fig. 4.41b runs all the way through from perimeter to perimeter.) Spiral clusters are frequently found among devotees of the golden section. Such an arrangement is not found anywhere in Palladio, for it cannot coexist with the technique of splitting.

Figure 4.42 reproduces one of the most Palladian designs from James Gibbs's influential *Book of Architecture* (1728). The facade is fully in one of our sixteen styles—a center composition block plus attic—though the quoins, corbels, and window frames (treated with "Gibbs surrounds") give it a heavily British look. And the plan is definitely quirky. The staircases are not symmetrically sized and the windows do not line up with the interior doors. Other Gibbs houses are much more obviously non-Palladian. Many of his plans do not have rectangular perimeters but jog in and out in a resolutely post-Palladian fashion (fig. 4.43), or else they have interior corridors (fig. 4.44), a feature never found in Palladio.

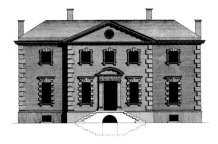

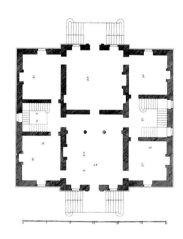

4.42   James Gibbs, house for a gentleman
in Oxfordshire, from Gibbs's A Book of
Architecture (1728).

4.43   James Gibbs, design for Sir Gregory
Page's house, Park Terrace, Greenwich,
London, 1720, from A Book of Architecture.

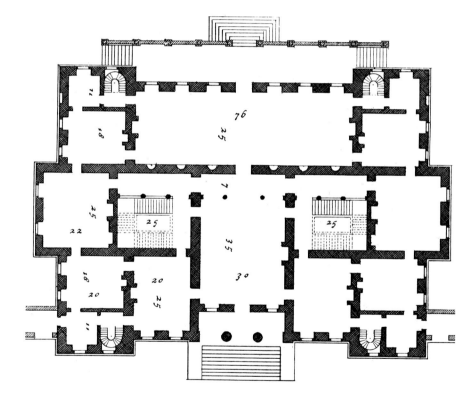

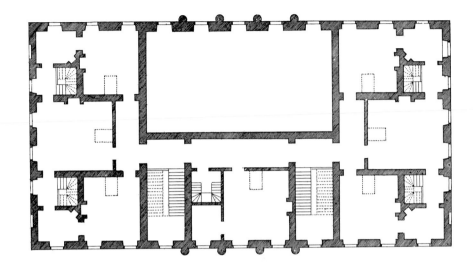

4.44 *James Gibbs, design for Sacombe Park, Hertfordshire, from* A Book of Architecture.

4.45 *Lord Burlington, plan and elevation of Chiswick House, Middlesex, 1723–1729, from William Kent,* The Designs of Inigo Jones *(1727).*

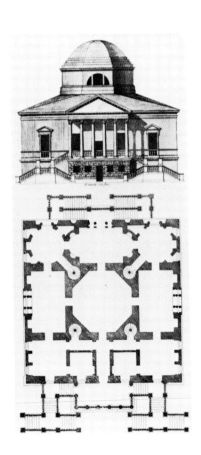

The most exalted and sedulously imitative Palladian in Great Britain was of course Lord Burlington. Yet consciously or unconsciously he was as loose in his interpretations of his master's rules as any of the other architects we have discussed—indeed more so. Both in plan and facade, Burlington's famous villa at Chiswick (fig. 4.45) utterly abandons Palladianism as we define it. The octagonal drum for the dome is heterodox—borrowed, it is often pointed out, from Scamozzi's Villa Pisani (fig. 4.37). Equally un-Palladian are the various elaborate multiaxial arrangements for front steps that were built or planned.[7] Much more non-Palladian, not to say anti-Palladian, is the basic conception, in plan, of the wall-to-volume structure. Palladio designed buildings composed of uniformly thick walls surrounding rectangular (and, very occasionally, cylindrical) rooms. Chiswick, in contrast, goes back to the tradition of Bramante and Michelangelo, as revived in the age of the Baroque: it is essentially a set of volumes carved out of a solid mass, as in a cave or rock-cut temple. Indeed, if we take account of the thick window embrasures and other ways of funneling light into the rooms, we have in Chiswick an essentially seventeenth-century arrangement of heterogeneous geometrical shapes: octagons, a cylinder, a double-apsed rectangle, plain

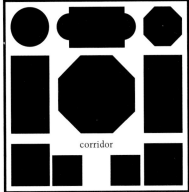

corridor

4.46   *Constituent shapes in the plan of Chiswick.*

4.47   *Thomas Jefferson, plan of Monticello, 1796 version. Courtesy Photograph Collection, Art and Architecture Library, Yale University.*

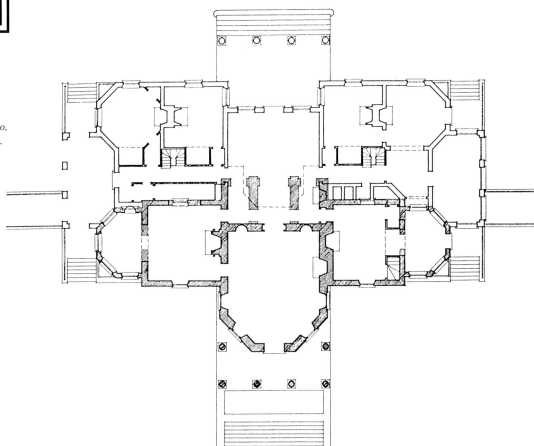

Chiswick   Monticello

4.48   *Transforming Chiswick into*
Monticello.

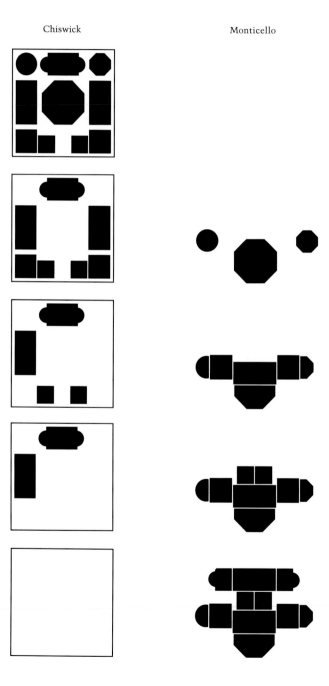

rectangles, and squares (fig. 4.46). Burlington also includes a circulation space that verges on being that supremely un-Palladian feature, an interior corridor.

America's own great Palladian architect, Thomas Jefferson, was no doubt inspired by the *Quattro Libri* as well as by some of the many books it spawned.[8] The earliest versions of the design for Monticello date from 1771. The plan, however, which underwent changes over time, is less indebted to Palladio than it is to the anti-Palladian Chiswick.[9] Indeed one can recreate the plan of Monticello, at least in the 1796 version (fig. 4.47), by reshuffling Chiswick's component room shapes into Monticello's distributions (fig. 4.48). Allowing for overlaps, the proportions and number of the shapes remain unchanged. Chiswick's central octagon establishes the thrust half-octagon portico in the center of Jefferson's house. Chiswick's two larger square rooms turn into Monticello's two front chambers. Burlington's two smaller square rooms, at the rear, then become Jefferson's two rear chambers. The Chiswick cylinder and small octagon melt into Monticello's front rooms to make the larger polygonal bays on the forward sides of Monticello. And the apses of Chiswick's rectangular hall do the same for Monticello's rear chambers.[10] The two lateral rectangles at Chiswick, finally, are rotated and placed one on top of the other to become the central spaces of Jefferson's house.

The discussion could be continued, but by now our point is made. By distinguishing between the certain, the possible, and the impossible, by showing how Palladio salted his firmest rules with statistically measurable doses of preference, we claim to have defined the layout and facade of the Palladian villa better than has been done so far. To us, in fact, these ideas comprise something that can be developed further. We believe we have found a new way of analyzing architectural design, a way not based solely on an architect's numerically limited accomplishments, however brilliant, but on the far greater realm of possibilities that may be rigorously extrapolated from those accomplishments.

APPENDIX

An English Translation of the "Aggionta del Palladio"

PROPOSED INSERT IN BOOK I OF

THE *QUATTRO LIBRI* (C. 1570).

FROM LIONELLO PUPPI, ED., *ANDREA*

PALLADIO: SCRITTI SULL'ARCHITET-

TURA (1554–1579) (VICENZA, 1988).

Having spoken in great detail, throughout this first book, of the orders of architecture and of the components of each of them in particular, it would be well to add another procedure that is used both for new work and for that which is to be added to existing work. For, with a given height either in a house already built that one wants to remodel, or in a house to be built new, it is necessary to know the rule to be followed in making the heights of the stories, and then the bases, capitals, and column heights; and what height the architraves, friezes, and cornices will have to be, so that from this rule anyone can then work out the extent of the architecture for himself according to his necessities and desires. . . . Here one has to take two considerations into account, [one for] the facades [and the other for] the ornamentation which is to be put to hand upon them. Speaking first of the facades, if they are to be made new, and if there are two stories, the lower will have to be one-fifth higher than the upper, and if there are three stories the top one should be one-sixth less than the middle one. With this proportion, experience shows, one gets a symmetry of great satisfaction to the eye, not different from that [one sees in] reeds which, the higher they grow, the shorter their blossoms are, seeing that taller things show greater weakness, and therefore [the blossoms] must be more densely grouped. If one has to remodel an old building, and these proportions do not exist in the story heights, the remodeled facade components can be improved by using proportions that give the effect of new work rather than of old work remodeled. The area from the base to the top of the lower story is divided into eleven modules, and the thickness of the column will be one module, the architrave, frieze, and cornice two, the column with base and capital nine, and this order should be Ionic. The second story must be divided into twelve modules, with the thickness of the column one, the architrave, frieze, and cornice two, and the base, shaft, and capital ten, which latter should be Corinthian. The third-story order should be Composite, and be divided into twelve modules with the subdivisions as in the Corinthian order, and with the proviso that, in all three orders, in order to raise the bases of the columns, the architect may at his discretion insert a pedestal, in which case the column bases must not have pedestals of their own. Thus are the orders more enjoyable. And this is enough for him who would understand the necessary art of the facade.

Now we come to the ornaments of the chambers and halls. Immediately under the ceiling beams I usually put the architrave, so that the beam [along the wall] can serve as a frieze, which is reasonable; and this architrave should be three-quarters of a module high, dividing the wall, from the level of the [storage] chests [lining the walls] up to the level just under the beams, into ten modules: but since current taste is not content with reasonableness in art, but wants to surpass normal good practice, many people want a cornice, frieze, and architrave under the ceiling; so, to give a rule also for this, so that one makes it as much in accordance with art as possible, the entire space of the wall of the room or chamber, from the chests or benches or *scagni* up to the beams, is divided into three parts, and one of these parts should be the height of the architrave, frieze, and cornice, with five for the column and its members; and the height of the chests can serve as a basement or if you like pedestal, according as it seems right to him who does the work.

NOTES

INTRODUCTION

1. The key book here is still Rudolf Wittkower, *Architectural Principles in the Age of Humanism* (London, 1949, with many reprints and several new editions). Other particularly relevant works are Erik Forssman, *Visible Harmony: Palladio's Villa Foscari at Malcontenta* (Stockholm, 1973); James S. Ackerman, *Palladio's Villas* (New York, 1967); L. Puppi, "Il trattato di Palladio e la sua fortuna in Italia e all'estero," *Bollettino del Centro Italiano di Studi d'Architettura 'A. Palladio'* [hereafter *Bollettino CISA*] 12 (1970), 257ff.; G. G. Zorzi, "La interpretazione dei disegni palladiani," *Bollettino CISA* 10 (1968), 97ff.; Robert Streitz, *Palladio: la Rotonde et sa géometrie* (Lausanne, 1973); Colin Rowe, "The Mathematics of the Ideal Villa: Palladio and Le Corbusier Compared," *Architectural Review* 142 (1967), 101ff.; Manfredo Tafuri, "L'idea di architettura nella letteratura teorica del manierismo," *Bollettino CISA* 9 (1967), 369ff.; Roberto Pane, "I Quattro Libri," *Bollettino CISA* 9 (1967), 121ff.; V. Fontana, "Il 'Vitruvio' del 1556: Barbaro, Palladio e Marcolini," in *Trattati scientifici nel Veneto tra il XV e il XVI secolo. Saggi e studi* (Venice, 1985); D. H. Feinstein, "Palladio und das Problem der musikalischen Proportionen in Architektur," in *Anreger durch vier Jahrhunderte: Palladio. Freiburger Universitätsblatt* (Freiburg, 1988), 39ff.; G. Barbieri, "La strategia della regola vivente: 'I Quattro Libri dell'Architettura' di Andrea Palladio," *Bollettino CISA* 22 (1980),

35ff.; D. Gioseffi, "I disegni dei 'Quattro Libri' come modelli, modellistica architettonica e teoria dei modelli," *Bollettino CISA* 22 (1980), 47ff.; Andrea Palladio, *I Quattro Libri dell'Architettura*, ed. L. Magagnato and P. Marini (Milan, 1980); L. Puppi, "Gli 'altri' libri dell'architettura di Andrea Palladio," *Bollettino CISA* 22 (1980), 65ff. See also note 10 below. For Palladio generally, see Deborah Howard, "Four Centuries of Literature on Palladio," *Journal of the Society of Architectural Historians* 39 (1980), 224ff., and the bibliography in Lionello Puppi, ed., *Andrea Palladio: Scritti sull'architettura (1554–1579)* (Vicenza, 1988).

2. M. M. Willcock, "Mythological Paradeigma in the *Iliad*," *Classical Quarterly* 58 (1964), 141ff.

3. Eugene O'Neill, Jr., "The Localization of Metrical Word-Types in the Greek Hexameter: Homer, Hesiod and the Alexandrians," *Yale Classical Studies* 8 (1942), 102ff. Hildebrecht Hommel has shown in a similar way that Aeschylus, in choruses from *Prometheus*, 526ff., made the antistrophes echo the strophes foot for foot, though the words were entirely different. Thus does the first line consist of a choriambus foot followed by an ionicus, the second line of a baccheus followed by another choriambus, and so on, line after line, all the way through. (Hildebrecht Hommel, *Symmetrie im Spiegel der Antike, Sitzungberichte der Heidelberger Akademie der Wissenschaften, Philosophische-Historische Klasse* [Heidelberg, 1987].)

4. See G. G. Zorzi, "La preparazione de 'I Quattro libri' . . .," in *I disegni delle antichità di*

Andrea Palladio (Venice, 1959), 145ff., and Puppi, *Andrea Palladio: scritti sull'architettura.* For the history of the book's preparation by Palladio, see Lionello Puppi, *Andrea Palladio* (Boston, 1973), 441ff.

5. But we must object to the use of the term "harmonic proportions" to refer to series other than the harmonic proper (as in "arithmetical, geometric, and harmonic series"). In the present case it is better to speak of "musical" ratios.

6. Wittkower's work first appeared as articles in the *Journal of the Warburg and Courtauld Institutes,* before its publication as a book in 1949.

7. L. Combes, "Packing Rectangles into Rectangular Arrangements," *Environment and Planning B* 3 (1976), 3ff.; W. J. Mitchell, J. P. Steadman, and Robin H. Liggett, "Synthesis and Optimization of Rectangular Floor Plans," *Environment and Planning B* 3 (1976), 37ff.; G. Stiny and W. J. Mitchell, "The Palladian Grammar," *Environment and Planning B* 5 (1978), 5ff.; G. Stiny and J. Gips, "An Evaluation of Palladian Plans," *Environment and Planning B* 5 (1978), 37ff., 200ff.; G. Stiny and W. J. Mitchell, "Counting Palladian Plans," *Environment and Planning B* 5 (1978), 189ff.

8. G. L. Hersey, *Pythagorean Palaces: Magic and Architecture in the Italian Renaissance* (Ithaca, 1976), 19ff.

9. L. March and G. Stiny, "Spatial Systems in Architecture and Design: Some History and Logic," *Environment and Planning B: Planning and Design* 12 (1985), 31ff.

10. Deborah Howard and Malcolm Longair, "Harmonic Proportion and Palladio's *Quattro Libri,*" *Journal of the Society of Architectural Historians* 41 (1982), 116ff. A recent rejoinder to the Howard and Longair article is Branko Mitrovic, "Palladio's Theory of Proportions and the Second Book of the *Quattro Libri,*" *Journal of the Society of Architectural Historians* 49 (1990), 279ff.

11. Howard and Longair, "Harmonic Proportion," 123.

12. Counting every ratio cited in this section, he gives: 5:3, 3:2, √2:1, 4:3, 3:1, 7:2, 4:1, 9:1, 5:1, 1:1, 2:1, 5:2, 9:8.

13. Marcus Vitruvius Pollio, *I dieci libri dell'architettura tradotti e commentati da Daniele Barbaro, 1567,* introduction by Manfredo Tafuri (Milan, 1987).

14. Mitrovic, "Palladio's Theory," 281. Our own discussion of these musical matters is indebted to Claude V. Palisca, *Humanism in Italian Renaissance Musical Thought* (New Haven, 1985), 35ff., 235ff.

15. Also, Renaissance scales such as the Pythagorean contained unwieldy ratios such as 64:81 (for a major third, C–E) and 128:243 (for a major seventh, C–B). In the rough and ready world of Renaissance villa design such values are hopelessly impractical. The first interval would have to be rounded off to 4:5 and the second probably to 1:2. Changing 128:243 into 1:2 transforms a major seventh into an octave, and hence turns a powerful dissonance into a consonance.

16. Palladio himself designed no rooms based on the "dissonant" ratios 8:9 and 128:243—respectively, in music, C–D (a major second) and C–B (a major seventh). Howard and Longair express surprise at this (p. 136), but perhaps he was reflecting musical practice in this negative way. In any event, the authors cite no

sixteenth-century precedents for their 34 "harmonic whole numbers," i.e., the privileged dimensions they derive from the musical intervals. As Mitrovic points out (p. 289), the idea that a given number may be "harmonic" in and of itself is foreign to the thought of the period. Only a ratio, not a single number, could be "harmonic."

17. Palladio, *Quattro Libri*, 1.52. All references to this work will be by book and chapter numbers.

18. Even the 3:5 can be worked in if we transform the major sixth from a dissonance to a consonance, which we can do if we adopt the new tuning proposed by the sixteenth-century theorist Ludovico Fogliano. (Wittkower, *Architectural Principles*, 133ff.)

19. A root-2 room based on a 32-foot square would measure 32×45.25; a 2:3 room of the same type would measure 32×48 and a 3:4 room 32×42.67—a difference hard to sense unless one room of each type were built side by side.

20. Howard and Longair, "Harmonic Proportion," 136.

21. *Quattro Libri*, 2.5.

22. See Combes, "Packing Rectangles."

23. But see William J. Mitchell, *Computer-Aided Architectural Design* (New York, 1977), 472, for a discussion of how to give dimensions to a "dimensionless" plan.

24. March and Stiny, "Spatial Systems," fig. 16.

25. Stiny and Gips, "An Evaluation," fig. 2. The authors write (p. 199): "the evaluative criteria considered do not depend on the actual dimensions of rooms in plans and hence do not incorporate any system of proportions. Rather, the evaluative criteria are based on the arrangements of rooms in plans and the shapes and sizes of these rooms in terms of an underlying grid." This seems to mean that location is taken into account but not shape. Squares and their multiples do duty for the many other shapes we find in Palladian plans. The Stiny-Gips plans are not truly plans, then, but maps. They show only that a hall, for example, is on the building's central axis and that it is symmetrically flanked by three vertically set smaller rooms; the diagram does not pretend to establish the rooms' shapes or relative sizes.

26. Sebastiano Serlio, *Tutta l'architettura di Sebastiano Serlio* (Venice, 1619). The book was published in parts starting in 1537.

27. Stiny and Mitchell, "The Palladian Grammar"; W. J. Mitchell, *The Logic of Architecture* (Cambridge, Mass., 1990); Philip Steadman, *Architectural Morphology* (New York, 1983).

28. Thus "when I was going to school in 1970" does not mean quite the same thing as "when I went to school in 1970," since the first phrase implies the idea of repeatedly showing up at school and the second does not have this implication.

1   THE BACKGROUND:
PALLADIO AND SYMMETRY

1. Rudolf Wittkower, *Architectural Principles in the Age of Humanism* (1949; rpt. New York, 1971), 70.

2. The best book on symmetry is Hermann Weyl, *Symmetry* (Princeton, 1952). For earlier works on the subject see Weyl's bibliography, plus J. D. Bernal, "Art and the Scientist,"

Circle: International Review of Constructive Art, 1938, 119ff. Also: Dagobert Frey, "Zum Problem der Symmetrie in der bildenden Kunst," Studium Generale 2 (1949), 268ff.; Rolf Wedewer, Zur Sprachlichkeit von Bildern (Cologne, 1985); Symmetrie in Kunst, Natur und Wissenschaft (exhibition catalogue, Darmstadt, 1986), a splendid set of essays, among which, for our purposes, Hans-Georg Sperlich's "Beruhrungen zwischen Symmetrie und Macht in der Architektur," 1:273ff., is particularly good; see also Hildebrecht Hommel's wittily named Symmetrie im Spiegel der Antike. Sitzungberichte der Heidelberger Akademie der Wissenschaften, Philosophische-Historische Klasse (Heidelberg, 1987); Giuseppe Cagliote, Simmetrie infrante nella scienza e nell'arte (Milan, 1983); J. Lee Kavanau, Symmetry, an Analytical Treatment (Los Angeles, 1980); Douglas Hofstadter, Gödel, Escher, Bach (New York, 1979); Roger Caillois, Equilibre et dissymétrie dans la nature et dans l'art (Oxford, 1971); Claus Möller, Symmetrie und Ornament (eine Analyse mathematischer Strukturen der darstellenden Kunst), Rhenische-Westfälische Akademie der Wissenschaften, Vorträge 339 (1984); Karl Lothar Wolf and D. Kuhn, Gestalt und Symmetrie. Eine Systematik der symmetrischen Körper (1952); the journal Symmetrie 1 (1986); S. Ferri, "Simmetria," Enciclopedia dell'arte antica 7 (1956), 575ff.; E. H. Gombrich, The Sense of Order: A Study in the Psychology of Decorative Art (London, 1979).

3. Walter Kambartel, Symmetrie und Schönheit. Über mögliche Voraussetzungen des neueren Kunstbewusstseins in der Architekturtheorie Claude Perraults (Munich, 1972). Kambartel claims that Perrault, in his 1683 Ordonnance des cinq espèces de colonnes, was the first to claim that modern symmetry was different from ancient (Kambartel, 37ff.). But after carefully reading this and the other texts Kambartel cites, it does not seem to us that bilateral mirror reflection, which is our general definition of symmetry, is clearly meant by these authors. Alberti defines "symmetry" as we would define "commensurability" (De re aedificatoria, 1.2, 4). He does, however, describe modern symmetry, if rather indirectly, when he writes: "Let us look at nature. If a dog has one ear that projects like that of a donkey, or if a man has one foot bigger than the other, or one hand very large and the other very small, we would designate this as defomity. . . . We see from all this how important it is in nature that left well correspond to right . . . and that [in architecture] the left and right sides, the upper and lower halves, and all similar divisions should correspond just as in an [animal] body" (Alberti, De re aedificatoria, 9.7). He also instances the open pages of a printed book with their neat corresponding rows and blocks of print.

4. Lisa Golombek and Donald Wilber, The Timurid Architecture of Iran and Turan (Princeton, 1988).

5. Leonardo was in Milan, interesting himself in architecture and almost certainly making contact with Francesco di Giorgio and Bramante, in the later 1480s. From this period comes the volume known as Ms. B, dated c. 1490, along with other architectural manuscripts, which together contain most of his plans and views of symmetrical churches.

Carlo Pedretti, *A Chronology of Leonardo da Vinci's Architectural Studies after 1500* (Geneva, 1962), 11. For the Milan of Francesco di Giorgio, Bramante, and Cesariano, see also Arnaldo Bruschi, *Bramante architetto* (Bari, 1969), 20ff.

6. Kambartel, *Symmetrie und Schönheit*, 44.

7. Quoted by Kambartel, *Symmetrie und Schönheit*, 47. From Claude Perrault, *Les dix livres d'architecture de Vitruve, corrigez et traduits nouvellement en françoys, etc.* (Paris, 1673), 10, n. 41.

8. Kambartel, *Symmetrie und Schönheit*, 18.

9. As Palladio was to do; Filarete means, in Greek, "lover of excellence" and Palladio means "devotee of Pallas."

10. Filarete [Antonio Averlino], *Trattato di architettura*, ed. Anna Maria Finoli and Liliana Grassi (Milan, 1972), 1:323ff., 2: pl. 61.

11. For further discussion see G. L. Hersey, *Pythagorean Palaces: Magic and Architecture in the Italian Renaissance* (Ithaca, 1976), 132ff.

12. Francesco di Giorgio Martini, *Trattati di architettura, ingegneria e arte militare*, ed. Corrado Maltese (Milan, 1967), 79.

13. For several illustrations and further discussion of Francesco as a planner, see Hersey, *Pythagorean Palaces*, 69ff.

14. These are all assumptions based on a rough sketch made by Baldassare Peruzzi when he visited Poggioreale early in the sixteenth century. For the most recent discussion with full bibliography on Poggioreale see David Marshall, "A View of Poggioreale by Viviano Codazzi and Domenico Gargiulo," *Journal of the Society of Architectural Historians* 45 (1986), 32ff. To his bibliography should be added Ludovica Trezzani's entry on Viviano Codazzi's *Festa nella villa di Poggioreale* (Besançon, Musée des Beaux-Arts), no. 2.39 in the exhibition catalogue *Civiltà del Seicento a Napoli* (Naples, Capodimonte, 1984).

15. George L. Hersey, *Alfonso II and the Artistic Renewal of Naples, 1485–1495* (New Haven, 1969), 58ff.

16. Sebastiano Serlio, *Tutte l'opere d'architettura et prospettiva* (Venice, 1619; rpt. Ridgewood, N.J., 1964), folio 122r.

17. Fritz Schreiber, *Die französische Renaissance-Architektur und die Poggio-Reale Variationen des Sebastiano Serlio* (Halle, 1938).

18. Lionello Puppi, "Un letterato in villa: Giangiorgio Trissino a Cricoli," *Arte veneta*, 1971, 72ff.

19. Palladio, *Quattro Libri*, 2.19.

20. Weyl, *Symmetry*, 109ff.

21. Palladio, *Quattro Libri*, 1.52.

22. Palladio, *Quattro Libri*, 2.76.

23. A Vicentine foot (the foot as measured in Palladio's town of Vicenza) was normally 13.5 US inches or 34.5 centimeters, though authorities, ancient and modern, disagree.

24. Martin Kubelik, "Palladio's Villas in the Tradition of the Veneto Farm," *Assemblage* 1 (1986), 91ff., and *Die Villa im Veneto. Zur typologischen Entwicklung im Quattrocento* (Munich, 1977), passim. On the other hand, Philip Goy shows that Renaissance houses erected in the villages around the Venetian Lagoon are generally quite symmetrical, even when unpretentious. Philip J. Goy, *Venetian Vernacular Architecture* (London, 1989).

25. Weyl, *Symmetry*, 66. See also L. March and G. Stiny, "Spatial Systems in Architecture and Design," *Environment and Planning B: Plan-*

ning and Design 12 (1985), 31, and Philip Steadman, "Modelling Leonardo's Ideas by Computer," in *Leonardo da Vinci* (New Haven and London, 1989), 209ff. and esp. 216ff.

26. Wolfgang Lotz, "Notes on the Centralized Church of the Renaissance," in *Studies in Italian Renaissance Architecture* (Cambridge, Mass., 1977), 66ff.

27. There are exceptions, e.g., the so-called garden houses at Ostia, which are laid out with two right-angled axes and bilateral reflection on both sides. But this applies only to the four-way groupings of the living units; the individual units are not symmetrical. See Carol Martin Watts and Donald J. Watts, "Geometrical Ordering of the Garden Houses at Ostia," *Journal of the Society of Architectural Historians* 46 (1987), 265ff. For Roman house plans generally, see A. G. McKay, *Houses, Villas and Palaces in the Roman World* (Ithaca, 1975).

28. Of course it can be argued that the asymmetry of Roman houses could hardly have been known in the Renaissance. The state of archaeology at that time made it possible to assume that Roman houses were on the whole symmetrical, modular, what you will. The point, however, is that they were not that way and that Vitruvius never claims that they were, nor that they should have been.

29. Tancredi Carunchio, *Origini della villa rinascimentale. La ricerca di una topologia* (Rome, 1974), passim.

30. Erik Forssman, "Palladio e Vitruvio," *Bollettino CISA* 4 (1962), 31ff.

31. It is interesting, in this connection, that Aristotle brands the $\sqrt{2}$:1 rectangle "asymmetrical," presumably because its length is not commensurable with its width.

32. Cesare Cesariano, ed. and trans., *Di Lucio Vitruvio Pollione de architectura libri decem* (Como, 1521), 49r, 50r.

33. And he is quite right. One can even add that the oldest and most primary meaning of *aedes* is "human habitation." The word "edifice" comes from *aedes* and *facere*, "to make an *aedes*."

34. Cesariano, *Vitruvio*, 48v.

35. Actually Ovid means that the nobles opened their *atria*, and their *atria* only, to the common people on certain festivals. But *atria* in the plural could also mean a whole palace, e.g., Ovid, *Fasti*, 3.703, where the word refers to the whole of Jove's palace. We thank Gordon Williams for these insights.

36. Vitruvius, *I dieci libri dell'architettura tradotti e commentati da Daniele Barbaro, 1567*, introduction by Manfredo Tafuri (Milan, 1987), xii. Hereafter cited as Barbaro. See also Vincenzo Fontana, "Il 'Vitruvio' del 1556: Barbaro, Palladio e Marcolini," in *Trattati scientifici nel Veneto tra il XV e il XVI secolo. Saggi e studi* (Venice, 1985), 39ff.; A. Corboz, "Una città sognata. Daniele Barbaro, Andrea Palladio e la pinata di Hochelaga," in Lionello Puppi, ed., *Palladio e Venezia* (Florence, 1982), 81ff.; Erik Forssman, "Palladio e Daniele Barbaro," *Bollettino CISA* 8 (1966), 68ff.

37. Barbaro, xv.

38. Barbaro, 282.

39. Barbaro, 289ff.

40. Barbaro, 121. This system generates a symmetrically splittable plan with regular compartments for the rooms (though the grid breaks down here and there), a main vertical axis made up of the third module, and a cross axis formed by the second module set verti-

cally. All of the major interior spaces are formed either by single occurrences of one of these modules or by clusters of them—though there is a good deal of overlapping or interlocking, viz.:

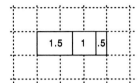

In the lower right-hand corner of the plan, the wing beside the portico is three 1-modules wide and the rooms therein are one 1-module deep, as indicated by the dotted lines in the diagram above. But, as we see from the heavy continuous lines that indicate the actual built walls, the room immediately flanking the portico is precisely one and a half 1-modules long. And the small room at the corner is precisely the vertically set half of a 1-module. The accuracy of these statements can be checked in Barbaro's book with a pair of dividers.

41. In his commentary on Vitruvius 6.2.1, furthermore, Barbaro, without actually saying that courtyards should be regular shapes, quotes his predecessor theorist, Leone Battista Alberti, on the courtyard as the generating heart of the house, which determines the surrounding rooms as a city piazza determines, or defines, the surrounding city.

42. The plan and elevation do not agree, for the elevation shows an octastyle portico and the plan a hexastyle.

43. Cicero, *Philippicae*, 2.110: "ut haberet pulvinar, simulacrum, fastigium, flaminem."

See also L. Annius Florus, *Epitome bellorum omnium annorum*, 2.13, 4.2.91.

44. L. B. Alberti, *De re aedificatoria* [1485], ed. G. Orlandi and P. Portoghesi (Milan, 1966), 2:809.

45. Nonetheless it is perfectly clear that Palladio had it in mind to present the image of an ancient Roman as opposed to a house of his own time. The facade is shown as partly ruined. For purposes of scale he shows only a fragment of the facade, but he makes it a literal fragment—a broken piece of wall from whose crannies sprout weeds. Also, we note, the masonry cladding has disappeared, revealing the brickwork of the inner walls.

46. Palladio illustrates further variations on the theme of the Roman house, complete with the various types of atrium mentioned by Vitruvius, in *Quattro Libri*, 2.24ff.

2   PLANMAKER

1. It is true that Palladio uses circular, cross-shaped, T-shaped, and I-shaped spaces, e.g., in the Villa Barbaro at Maser and in the Rotonda. But he never does so more than once in any plan, and does even that in fewer than half his plans. Generating these nonrectangular rooms turns out to be a knotty problem. We address it in chapter 4.

2. Due to adjustments made for the width of the villa's rather thick walls, room dimensions in the split tree do not correspond exactly to the dimensions in the original plan.

3. Palladio, *Quattro Libri*, 2.20. In his written directions for generating an Ionic entablature, Palladio inadvertently reverses the sizes of the first and third fascias. Instead of giving *five* parts to the first fascia, four to the second,

and *three* to the third, as he does correctly in his illustration, his text tells us to give *three* to the first, four to the second, and *five* to the third.

4. Palladio, *Quattro Libri*, 2.4.

5. In saying this, Palladio is only following Alberti, who in the fifteenth century had written: "Some [rooms] should be larger, as necessity dictates, like the inner courtyards, while others require a smaller area, like the chambers and all private apartments. Some others are medium, such as dining rooms and the vestibule." Leone Battista Alberti, *De re aedificatoria* (Florence, 1485), fols. 160r, 161v.

6. Palladio, *Quattro Libri*, 1.52.

7. Palladio, *Quattro Libri*, 2.55: a project, really a palazzo, for Count Giacomo Angarano.

8. Rudolf Wittkower, *Architectural Principles in the Age of Humanism* (London, 1967), 73.

9. Palladio, *Quattro Libri*, 1.1.

10. G. Stiny and W. J. Mitchell, "The Palladian Grammar," *Environment and Planning B* 5 (1978), 51–58. See also G. Stiny and W. J. Mitchell, "Counting Palladian Plans," *Environment and Planning B* 5 (1978), 189–198.

11. Palladio, *Quattro Libri*, 1.55.

3 FACADEMAKER

1. Compare H. Koning and J. Eizenberg, "The Language of the Prairie: Frank Lloyd Wright's Prairie Houses," *Environment and Planning B* 8 (1981), 295ff. Unlike Koning and Eizenberg, who used three-dimensional blocks to reconstruct the volumes of Frank Lloyd Wright's Prairie Style houses, we are not interested in the mass but rather in the two-dimensional facade.

2. We should note that art historians have long debated attributing the Villa Valmarana at Vigardolo (fig. 3.4c) to Palladio. As experimenters, however, we will include its graceful entrance among our possibilities.

3. The rear facade shown in figure 3.31 is based on the rear facade of the Villa Caldogno in Caldogno. We have shaded the pediments to make the illustration easier to read.

4 SOME CONCLUSIONS

1. Rudolf Wittkower, *Architectural Principles in the Age of Humanism* (London, 1967), 128.

2. Wittkower, *Architectural Principles*, 126ff.

3. Lionello Puppi, *Andrea Palladio* (Boston, 1973), catalogue beginning on p. 237.

4. For a history of the serliana see Rudolf Wittkower, *Palladio and English Palladianism* (London, 1974), 166ff. Also Stanislaw Wilinsky, "La serliana di Villa Pojana a Pojana Maggiore," *Bollettino CISA* 10 (1968), 79ff.

5. Colin Rowe, *The Mathematics of the Ideal Villa* (Cambrige, Mass., 1976), 7ff.

6. John Harris and Gordon Higgott, *Inigo Jones: The Complete Architectural Drawings* (London, 1989). Annarosa Cerutti Fusco, in *Inigo Jones, Vitruvius Britannicus: Jones e Palladio nella cultura architettonica inglese, 1600–1740* (Rimini, 1985), says that this facade was originally constructed by Isaac de Caus in 1636–1640, then rebuilt by Webb, after a fire, in 1649 (p. 371ff.).

7. Rudolf Wittkower, "Lord Burlington and William Kent," in Wittkower, *Palladio and English Palladianism* (London, 1974), 115ff.

8. See the catalogue by W. B. O'Neal, *Jefferson's Fine Arts Library* (Charlottesville, Va., 1976).

Jefferson owned at least six different editions of the *Quattro Libri* (see O'Neal, s.v. Palladio). See also Heinz Horat, "Thomas Jefferson: Intellectual Architecture," *Architectura*, 1989, no. 1, 62ff.; William Howard Adams, *Jefferson's Monticello* (New York, 1983); Gene Waddell, "The First Monticello," *Journal of the Society of Architectural Historians* 46 (1987), 8ff. Particularly important for Jefferson was Robert Morris's *Select Architecture* (1755), which combined Palladio's ideas about strictly symmetrical smaller houses with other geometrical constructs and with hints of Masonic symbolism.

9. Frederick D. Nichols and James A. Bear, Jr., *Monticello* (Monticello, Va., 1967).

10. Horat, "Thomas Jefferson," presents evidence that the polygonal apses were chosen because Jefferson feared that the local builders were incapable of cylindrical ones.

BIBLIOGRAPHY

Ackerman, James S. *Palladio Revisited*. New Orleans, 1981.

Ackerman, James S. *Palladio's Villas*. New York, 1967.

Adams, William Howard. *Jefferson's Monticello*. New York, 1983.

Alberti, Leone Battista. *De re aedificatoria* [1485], ed. G. Orlandi and P. Portoghesi. Milan, 1966.

Barbieri, G. "La strategia della regola vivente: 'I Quattro Libri dell'Architettura' di Andrea Palladio." *Bollettino CISA* 22 (1980), 35ff.

Basso, Don U. *La villa e il tempietto dei Barbaro a Maser di Andrea Palladio*. Montebelluna, 1976.

Battisti, Eugenio. "Un tentativo di analisi strutturali del Palladio tramite le teorie musicali del cinquecento e l'impiego di figure rettoriche." *Bollettino CISA* 15 (1973), 211ff.

Belli, Silvio. *Della proporzione e della proporzionalità communi passioni del quanto*. Venice, 1573.

Bernal, J. D. "Art and the Scientist." *Circle: International Review of Constructive Art*, 1938, 119ff.

Bolcano, V. "L'ambiente musicale a Vicenza e a Verona ai tempi del Palladio." In *Palladio e Verona*, exhibition catalogue. Verona, 1980.

Bruhns, L. "Von der Bedeutung der Symmetrie für die Didaktik römische Kunstwerke." *Historisches Jahrbuch der Görres-Gesellschaft* 72 (1952), 77ff.

Cagliote, Giuseppe. *Simmetrie infrante nella scienza e nell'arte*. Milan, 1983.

Caillois, Roger. *Equilibre et dissymétrie dans la nature et dans l'art*. Oxford, 1971.

Carunchio, Tancredi. *Origini della villa rinascimentale. La ricerca di una tipologia*. Rome, 1974.

Cerutti Fusco, Annarosa. *Inigo Jones, Vitruvius Britannicus: Jones e Palladio nella cultura architettonica inglese, 1600–1740*. Rimini, 1985.

Cesariano, Cesare, ed. and trans. *Di Lucio Vitruvio Pollione de architectura libri decem*. Como, 1521.

Combes, L. "Packing Rectangles into Rectangular Arrangements." *Environment and Planning B* 3 (1976), 3ff.

Corboz, A. "Una città sognata. Daniele Barbaro, Andrea Palladio e la pinata di Hochelaga oggi Montreal." In Lionello Puppi, ed., *Palladio e Venezia*. Florence, 1982

Engelhardt, W. von. "Sinn und Begriff der Symmetrie." *Studium Generale* 6 (1953), 524.

Feinstein, D. H. "Palladio und das Problem der musikalischen Proportionen in Architektur." In *Anreger durch vier Jahrhunderte: Palladio. Freiburger Universitätsblatt*. Freiburg, 1988.

Filarete [Antonio Averlino]. *Trattato di architettura*. Ed. Anna Maria Finoli and Liliana Grassi. Milan, 1972.

Fontana, V. "Il 'Vitruvio' del 1556: Barbaro, Palladio e Marcolini." In *Trattati scientifici nel Veneto tra il XV e il XVI secolo. Saggi e studi*. Venice, 1985.

Forssman, Erik. "Palladio e Daniele Barbaro." *Bollettino CISA* 8 (1966), 337ff.

Forssman, Erik. "Palladio e Vitruvio." *Bollettino CISA* 4 (1962), 31ff.

Forssman, Erik. "Palladios Lehrgebäude. Studien über den Zusammenhang von Architektur und Architekturtheorie bei Andrea Palladio." *Acta universitatis Stockholmensis*. Stockholm, 1965.

Forssman, Erik. *Visible Harmony: Palladio's Villa Foscari at Malcontenta*. Stockholm, 1973.

Freedman, Richard. "A Computer Recreation of Palladian Villa Plans." *Architectura*, 1987, no. 1, 58ff.

Frey, Dagobert. "Zum Problem der Symmetrie in der bildenden Kunst." *Studium Generale* 2 (1949), 268ff.

Friedman, Terry. *James Gibbs*. New Haven, 1984.

Gibbs, James. *A Book of Architecture*. London, 1728.

Gioseffi, D. "I disegni dei 'Quattro Libri' come modelli, modellistica architettonica e teoria dei modelli." *Bollettino CISA* 22 (1980), 47ff.

Goy, Richard J. *Venetian Vernacular Architecture*. London, 1989.

Harris, John. *The Palladians*. New York, 1982.

Harris, John, and Gordon Higgott. *Inigo Jones: The Complete Architectural Drawings*. London, 1989.

Hersey, George L. *Alfonso II and the Artistic Renewal of Naples, 1485–1495*. New Haven, 1969.

Hersey, George L. "Poggioreale: Notes on a Reconstruction, and an Early Replication." *Architectura* 1 (1973), 13ff.

Hersey, George. *Pythagorean Palaces: Magic and Architecture in the Italian Renaissance*. Ithaca, 1976.

Hofer, Paul. *Palladios Erstling. Die Villa Godi Valmarana in Lonedo bei Vicenza*. Basel and Stuttgart, 1969.

Hofstadter, Douglas. *Gödel, Escher, Bach: An Eternal Golden Braid.* New York, 1979.

Holburton, Paul. *Palladio's Villas: Life in the Renaissance Countryside.* London, 1990.

Hommel, Hildebrecht. *Symmetrie im Spiegel der Antike. Sitzungberichte der Heidelberger Akademie der Wissenschaften, Philosophische-Historische Klasse.* Heidelberg, 1987.

Horat, Heinz. "Thomas Jefferson: Intellectual Architecture." *Architectura,* 1989, no. 1, 62ff.

Howard, Deborah. "Four Centuries of Literature on Palladio." *Journal of the Society of Architectural Historians* 39 (1980), 224ff.

Howard, Deborah, and Malcolm Longair. "Harmonic Proportion and Palladio's *Quattro Libri." Journal of the Society of Architectural Historians* 41 (1982), 116ff.

Kambartel, Walter. "Symmetrie." In *Historisches Wörterbuch der Philosophie.* Basel and Stuttgart, 1971ff.

Kambartel, Walter. *Symmetrie und Schönheit. Über mögliche Voraussetzungen des neueren Kunstbewusstseins in der Architekturtheorie Claude Perraults.* Munich, 1972.

Koning, H., and J. Eizenberg. "The Language of the Prairie: Frank Lloyd Wright's Prairie Houses." *Environment and Planning B* 8 (1981), 295ff.

Krishnamurti, R., and P. H. O'N. Roe. "Algorithmic Aspects of Plan Generation and Enumeration." *Environment and Planning B* 5 (1978), 157ff.

Kubelik, Martin. "Palladio's Villas in the Tradition of the Veneto Farm." *Assemblage* 1 (1986), 91ff.

Kubelik, Martin. *Die Villa im Veneto. Zur typologischen Entwicklung im Quattrocento.* Munich, 1977.

Lancaster, Clay. "Jefferson's Architectural Indebtedness to Robert Morris." *Journal of the Society of Architectural Historians* 10 (1951), 2ff.

Lewis, Douglas. *The Drawings of Andrea Palladio.* Exhibition catalogue. Washington, D.C., 1981.

Lotz, Wolfgang. "Notes on the Centralized Church of the Renaissance." In his *Studies in Italian Renaissance Architecture.* Cambridge, Mass., 1977.

Lücke, Hans-Carl. *Alberti-Index. Leon Battista Alberti, De re aedificatoria, Florenz 1485. Index Verborum.* Munich, 1975.

McKay, A. G. *Houses, Villas and Palaces in the Roman World.* Ithaca, 1975.

March, L., and G. Stiny. "Spatial Systems in Architecture and Design: Some History and Logic." *Environment and Planning B* 12 (1985), 31ff.

Marder, Tod A. "Bernini and Alexander VII: Criticism and Praise of the Pantheon in the Seventeenth Century." *Art Bulletin* 71 (1989), 628ff.

Marshall, David. "A View of Poggioreale by Viviano Codazzi and Domenico Gargiulo." *Journal of the Society of Architectural Historians* 45 (1986), 32ff.

Martini, Francesco di Giorgio. *Trattati di architettura, ingegneria e arte militare.* Ed. Corrado Maltese. Milan, 1967.

Mazzotti, G. *Palladian and Other Venetian Villas.* 2d ed. 1966.

Mitchell, W. J., J. P. Steadman, and Robin H. Liggett. "Synthesis and Optimization of Rectangular Floor Plans." *Environment and Planning B* 3 (1976), 37ff.

Mitrovic, Branko. "Palladio's Theory of Proportions and the Second Book of the *Quattro Libri.*" *Journal of the Society of Architectural Historians* 49 (1990), 279ff.

Möller, Claus. *Symmetrie und Ornament (eine Analyse mathematischer Strukturen der darstellenden Kunst).* Rhenische-Westfälische Akademie der Wissenschaften, *Vorträge* 339 (1984).

Morresi, Manuela. *Villa Porto Colleoni a Thiene: architettura e committenza nel rinascimento.* Milan, 1988.

Nichols, Frederick D., and James A. Bear, Jr. *Monticello.* Monticello, Va., 1967.

Nicolle, J. "Questions rélatives à la symétrie." *Zeitschrift für Ästhetik und allgemeine Kunstwissenschaft* 14 (1969), 1, 8ff.

Nicolle, J. *La symétrie.* Paris, 1957.

Nicolle, J. *La symétrie dans la nature et les travaux des hommes.* Paris, 1955.

O'Neal, W. B. *Jefferson's Fine Arts Library.* Charlottesville, Va., 1976.

Palladio, Andrea. *I Quattro Libri dell'Architettura.* Ed. L. Magagnato and P. Marini. Milan, 1980.

Pane, Roberto. "I Quattro libri." *Bollettino CISA* 9 (1967), 121ff.

Puppi, Lionello. "Gli 'altri' libri dell'architettura di Andrea Palladio." *Bollettino CISA* 22 (1980), 65ff.

Puppi, Lionello. *Andrea Palladio.* Boston, 1973.

Puppi, Lionello, ed. *Andrea Palladio: scritti sull'architettura (1554–1579)*. Vicenza, 1988.

Puppi, Lionello. "Un letterato in villa: Giangiorgio Trissino a Cricoli." *Arte veneta*, 1971, 72ff.

Puppi, Lionello. "Il trattato di Palladio e la sua fortuna in Italia e all'estero." *Bollettino CISA* 12 (1970), 257ff.

Rowe, Colin. *The Mathematics of the Ideal Villa*. Cambridge, Mass., 1976.

Scamozzi, Vincenzo. *Idea della Architettura universale . . .* Venice, 1615.

Schreiber, Fritz. *Die französische Renaissance-Architektur und die Poggio-Reale Variationen des Sebastiano Serlio*. Halle, 1938.

Schumaker, Thomas. "The Palladio Variations: Reconciling Convention, Parti, and Space." *Cornell Journal of Architecture*, 1991, 13ff.

Seebohm, Thomas. "CAD and the Baroque." Pamphlet, School of Architecture, University of Waterloo, Waterloo, Ontario, 1989.

Seebohm, Thomas. "A Possible Palladian Villa." Pamphlet, School of Architecture, University of Waterloo, Waterloo, Ontario.

Serlio, Sebastiano. *Tutte l'opere d'architettura et prospettiva* [Venice, 1619]. Ridgewood, N.J., 1964.

Sperlich, Hans-Georg. "Beruhrungen zwischen Symmetrie und Macht in der Architektur." In *Symmetrie in Kunst, Natur und Wissenschaft*, exhibition catalogue. Darmstadt, 1986.

Steadman, Philip. "Modelling Leonardo's Ideas by Computer." In Martin Kemp, ed., *Leonardo da Vinci*. New Haven and London, 1989.

Stiny, G., and J. Gips. *Algorhythmic Aesthetics: Computer Models for Criticism and Design in the Arts*. Berkeley, 1978.

Stiny, G., and J. Gips. "An Evaluation of Palladian Plans." *Environment and Planning B* 5 (1978), 37ff., 200ff.

Stiny, G., and L. March. "Spatial Systems in Architecture and Design: Some History and Logic." *Environment and Planning B* 12 (1985), 31ff.

Stiny, G., and W. J. Mitchell. "Counting Palladian Plans." *Environment and Planning B* 5 (1978), 189ff.

Stiny, G., and W. J. Mitchell. "The Palladian Grammar." *Environment and Planning B* 5 (1978), 5ff.

Streitz, Robert. *Palladio: la Rotonde et sa géometrie*. Lausanne, 1973.

Tafuri, Manfredo. "Alle origini di Palladianesimo. Alessandro Farnese, Jacques Androuet du Cerceau, Inigo Jones." *Storia dell'arte* 11, 149ff.

Tafuri, Manfredo. "L'idea di architettura nella letteratura teorica del manierismo." *Bollettino CISA* 9 (1967), 369ff.

Tafuri, Manfredo. "La norma e il programma: il Vitruvio di Daniele Barbaro." In Vitruvius, *I dieci libri* (Milan, 1987).

Tavernor, Robert. *Palladio and Palladianism.* London, 1991.

Teague, Edward H. *Andrea Palladio: A Bibliography of Recent Literature.* Monticello, Va., 1989.

Tigler, Peter. *Die Architekturtheorie des Filarete.* Berlin, 1963.

Trager, Philip. *The Villas of Palladio.* Boston, 1986.

Trezzani, Ludovica. Entry on the painting by Viviano Codazzi, *Festa nella villa di Poggioreale* (Besançon, Musée des Beaux-Arts), no. 2.39 in the exhibition catalogue *Civiltà del Seicento a Napoli.* Naples, 1984.

Vitruvius (Marcus Vitruvius Pollio). *I dieci libri dell'architettura tradotti e commentati da Daniele Barbaro, 1567.* Introduction by Manfredo Tafuri. Milan, 1987.

Waddell, Gene. "The First Monticello." *Journal of the Society of Architectural Historians* 46 (1987), 8ff.

Watts, Carol Martin, and Donald J. Watts. "Geometrical Ordering of the Garden Houses at Ostia." *Journal of the Society of Architectural Historians* 46 (1987), 265ff.

Wedewer, Rolf. *Zur Sprachlichkeit von Bildern.* Cologne, 1985. Reprinted in *Symmetrie in Kunst, Natur und Wissenschaft*, exhibition catalogue. Darmstadt, 1986.

Weyl, Hermann. *Symmetry.* Princeton, 1952.

Wilinsky, Stanislaw. "La serliana di Villa Pojana a Pojana Maggiore." *Bollettino CISA* 10 (1968), 79ff.

Wille, Rudolf. "Symmetrie—Versuch einer Begriffsbestimmung." In *Symmetrie in Kunst, Natur und Wissenschaft*, exhibition catalogue. Darmstadt, 1986.

Wittkower, Rudolf. *Architectural Principles in the Age of Humanism.* London, 1949 (with many reprints and several new editions).

Wittkower, Rudolf. *Palladio and English Palladianism.* London, 1974.

Wolbert, Klaus. "Symmetrie als Sprachformen der Kunst." In *Symmetrie in Kunst, Natur und Wissenschaft*, exhibition catalogue. Darmstadt, 1986.

The villas of Palladio

HAVE BEEN AMONG THE MOST INFLUENTIAL BUILDINGS IN HISTORY. Drawing on the architect's original published legacy of forty-odd designs, George Hersey and Richard Freedman reveal the rigorous geometric rules by which Palladio conceived these structures.

Where most earlier attempts to analyze the villas are mere lists of numbers and ratios that ignore space distribution, the present rules produce actual designs. Using a computer, the authors test each rule in every possible application, establishing a degree of validity not possible in ad hoc analyses. Progressing from the architect's most obvious to his subtlest geometry, the computer ultimately creates villa plans and facades that are stylistically indistinguishable from those of Palladio himself.

Possible Palladian Villas opens the way to similar analyses of other such "paradigmatic" designs, whether Chinese screens, Greek temples, baroque churches, or Frank Lloyd Wright's Prairie Houses. In fact a new approach to architectural history emerges: we can study designs that a given master might have produced but did not. Palladio's actual buildings, along with those of his generations of imitators, are set into the context not only of a new theory but of a new type of theory.

Along with the Macintosh disk that runs the program, *Possible Palladian Villas* will fascinate the design community and students of architectural style, symmetry, and geometry.

George Hersey is Professor of the History of Art at Yale University. Richard Freedman, who designed the computer program, is a product marketer working on MS-DOS at the Microsoft Corporation.

Possible Palladian Villas: The Program

A separate disk is available that allows the user to design Palladian villas by applying the rules described in the book. The program is available only for Macintosh computers. It requires 512K memory, runs on any Macintosh system, and is compatible with System 7.

9 780262 581103   90000

HERPP